CURSE OF THE WENDIGO

NICK
JUAN
JOSEP
RICH W
JOSH JO
JASON U
JOSH GR
CHRIS CA

DYNAMITE
ENTERTAINMENT

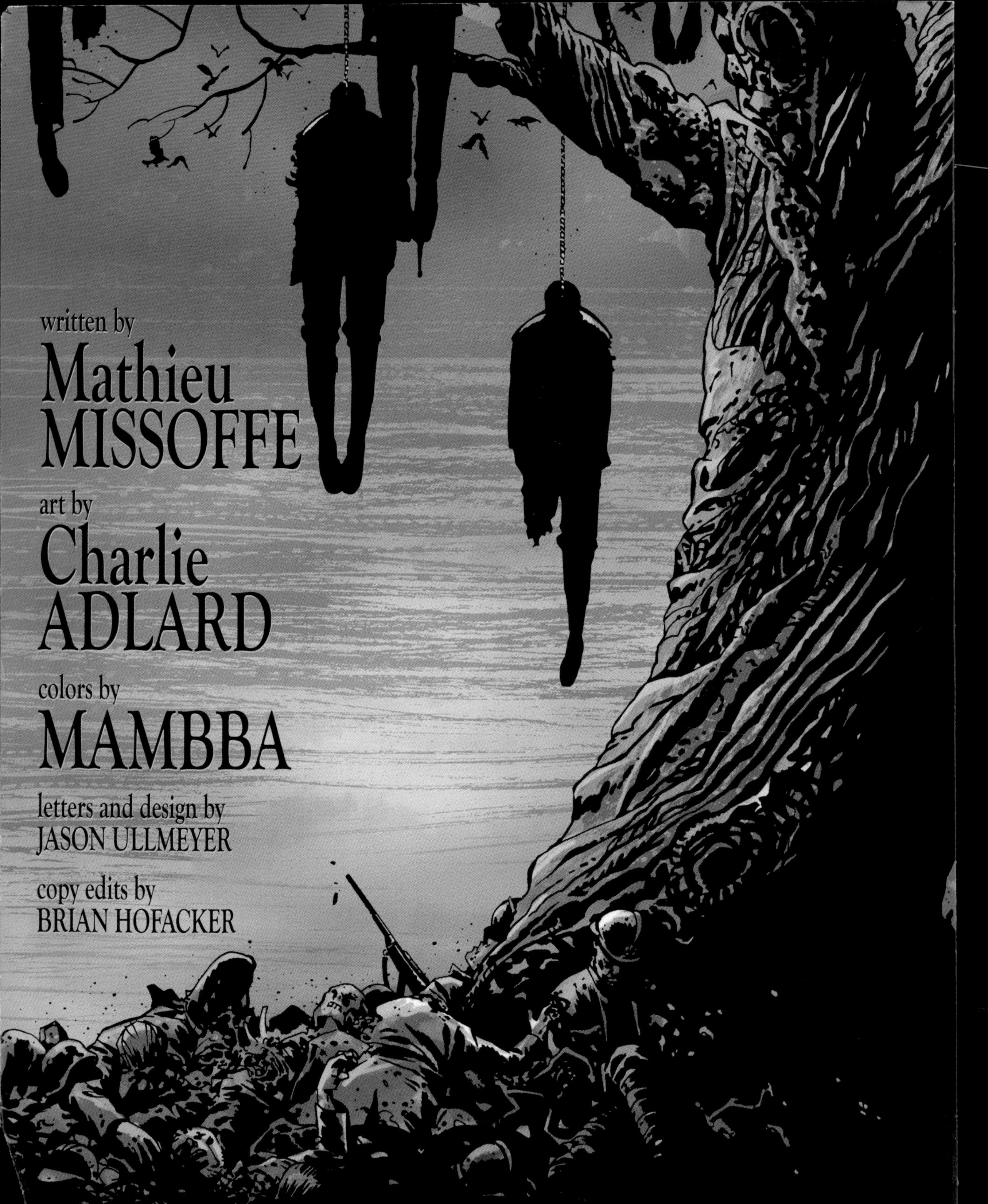

written by
Mathieu MISSOFFE

art by
Charlie ADLARD

colors by
MAMBBA

letters and design by
JASON ULLMEYER

copy edits by
BRIAN HOFACKER

DYNAMITE ENTERTAINMENT
WWW.DYNAMITE.NET

BARRUCCI	PRESIDENT
COLLADO	CHIEF OPERATING OFFICER
H RYBANDT	EDITOR
OUNG	DIRECTOR BUSINESS DEVELOPMENT
HNSON	CREATIVE DIRECTOR
LLMEYER	SENIOR DESIGNER
EN	TRAFFIC COORDINATOR
IANO	PRODUCTION ASSISTANT

First Edition ISBN-10: 1-60690-238-5 ISBN-13: 978-1-60690-238-7 10 9 8 7 6 5 4 3 2 1

For information regarding press, media rights, foreign rights, licensing, promotions, and advertising e-mail: marketing@dynamite.net

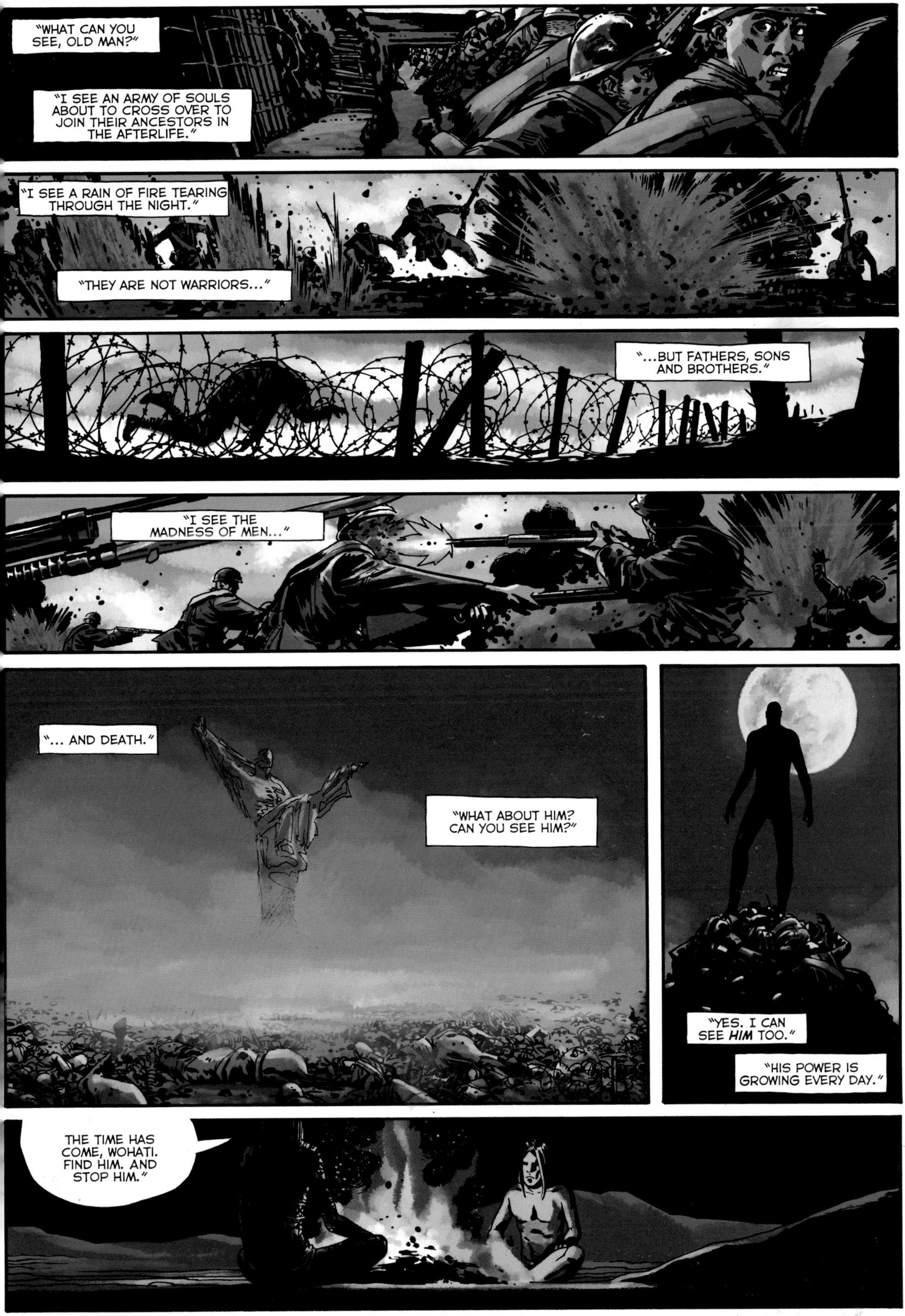
"WHAT CAN YOU SEE, OLD MAN?"
"I SEE AN ARMY OF SOULS ABOUT TO CROSS OVER TO JOIN THEIR ANCESTORS IN THE AFTERLIFE."
"I SEE A RAIN OF FIRE TEARING THROUGH THE NIGHT."
"THEY ARE NOT WARRIORS..."
"...BUT FATHERS, SONS AND BROTHERS."
"I SEE THE MADNESS OF MEN..."
"... AND DEATH."
"WHAT ABOUT HIM? CAN YOU SEE HIM?"
"YES. I CAN SEE *HIM* TOO."
"HIS POWER IS GROWING EVERY DAY."
THE TIME HAS COME, WOHATI. FIND HIM. AND STOP HIM."

NINE MONTHS LATER. FRENCH FLANDERS. JULY 1917.

ANYBODY IN THERE?

HEY, YOU! *INDIAN!*

FORGET IT, CLOVIS. HE'S NOT EXACTLY THE CHATTING TYPE.

NOT THAT YOU WOULD UNDERSTAND THAT REDSKIN'S LANGUAGE ANYWAY.

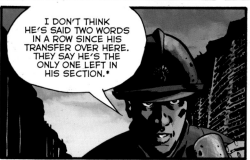

I DON'T THINK HE'S SAID TWO WORDS IN A ROW SINCE HIS TRANSFER OVER HERE. THEY SAY HE'S THE ONLY ONE LEFT IN HIS SECTION.*

MUST BE PRETTY SAD TO CROSS AN ENTIRE OCEAN ONLY TO DIE ON THE OTHER SIDE OF THE PLANET...

I WAS BORN 40 MILES AWAY FROM HERE, BUT THAT DOESN'T MAKE *ME* HAPPY TO DIE HERE EITHER.

DON'T WORRY, I'M SURE YOU'LL DO JUST FINE, CLOVIS.

WE WERE JUST TRYING TO CHEER UP THE NEWBIE, SERGEANT.

WHY DON'T YOU LEAVE HIM ALONE INSTEAD. HERE'S YOUR MAIL.

OPENED AND READ BY THE ENTIRE STAFF AS USUAL. AT LEAST THEY COULD CHECK MY MOTHER'S SPELLING...

SERGEANT CHÉREAU!!!

OUCH. SOUNDS LIKE THE LIEUTENANT FINALLY LEARNED ABOUT HIS WIFE IN TODAY'S MAIL...

*AN ESTIMATE OF MORE THAN 12,000 AMERICAN INDIANS FOUGHT IN THE TRENCHES DURING THE FIRST WORLD WAR. AT THAT TIME, THE UNITED STATES HAD NOT YET GRANTED THEM CITIZENSHIP.

4

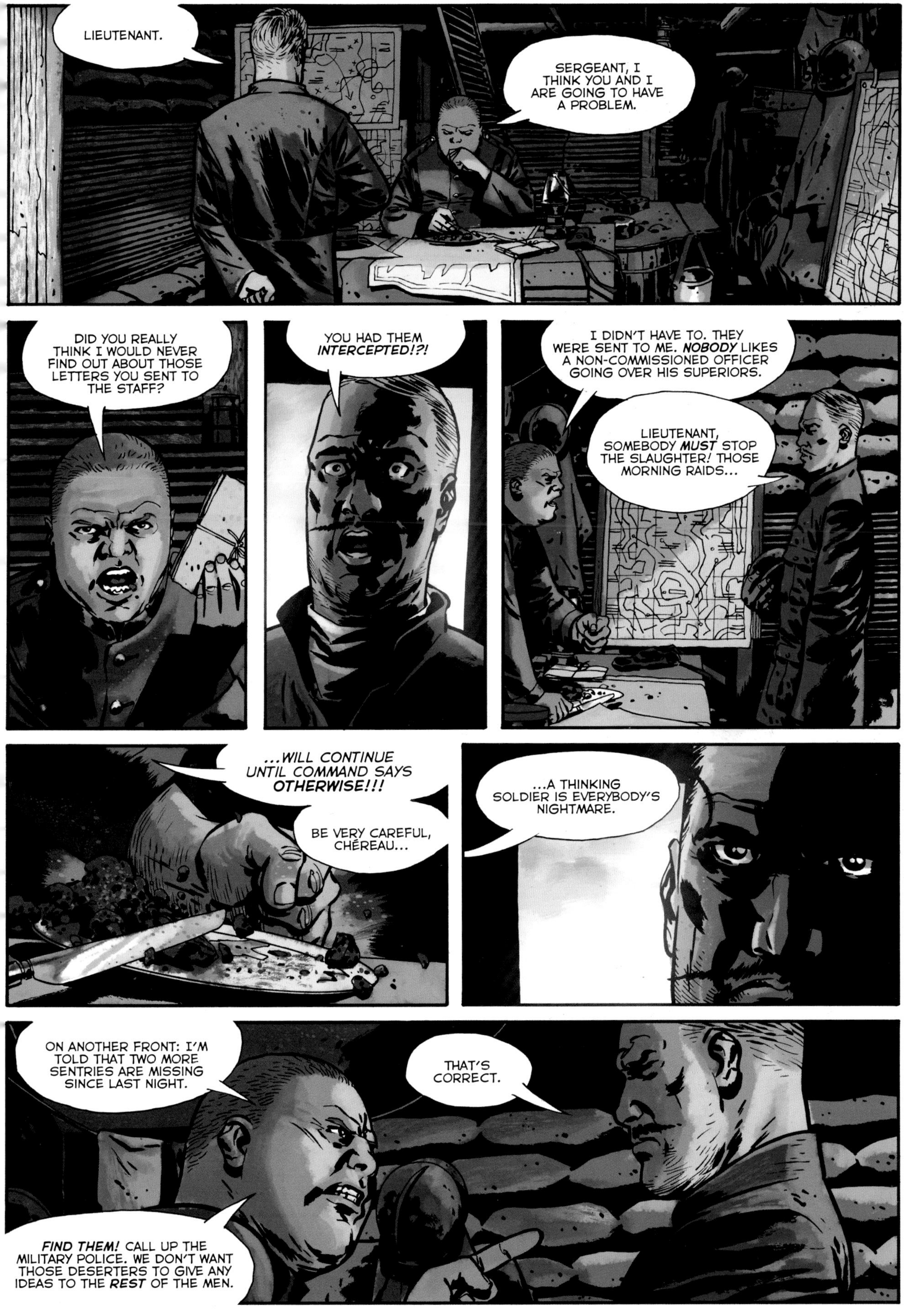
LIEUTENANT.
SERGEANT, I THINK YOU AND I ARE GOING TO HAVE A PROBLEM.
DID YOU REALLY THINK I WOULD NEVER FIND OUT ABOUT THOSE LETTERS YOU SENT TO THE STAFF?
YOU HAD THEM *INTERCEPTED!?!*
I DIDN'T HAVE TO. THEY WERE SENT TO ME. ***NOBODY*** LIKES A NON-COMMISSIONED OFFICER GOING OVER HIS SUPERIORS.
LIEUTENANT, SOMEBODY ***MUST*** STOP THE SLAUGHTER! THOSE MORNING RAIDS...
...WILL CONTINUE UNTIL COMMAND SAYS ***OTHERWISE!!!***
BE VERY CAREFUL, CHÉREAU...
...A THINKING SOLDIER IS EVERYBODY'S NIGHTMARE.
ON ANOTHER FRONT: I'M TOLD THAT TWO MORE SENTRIES ARE MISSING SINCE LAST NIGHT.
THAT'S CORRECT.
FIND THEM! CALL UP THE MILITARY POLICE. WE DON'T WANT THOSE DESERTERS TO GIVE ANY IDEAS TO THE ***REST*** OF THE MEN.

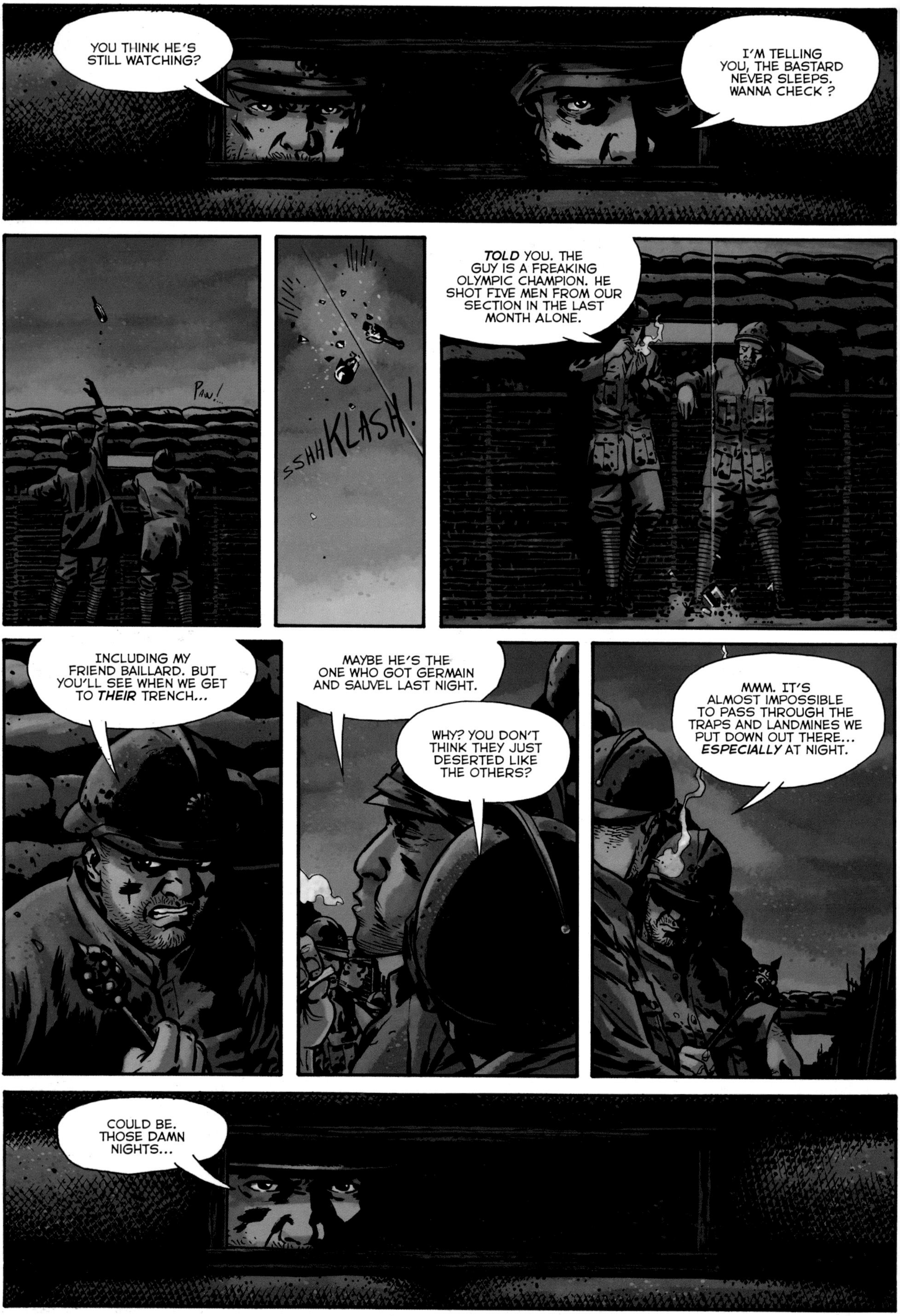
YOU THINK HE'S STILL WATCHING?
I'M TELLING YOU, THE BASTARD NEVER SLEEPS. WANNA CHECK ?
PAW!...
SSHHKLASH!
TOLD YOU. THE GUY IS A FREAKING OLYMPIC CHAMPION. HE SHOT FIVE MEN FROM OUR SECTION IN THE LAST MONTH ALONE.
INCLUDING MY FRIEND BAILLARD. BUT YOU'LL SEE WHEN WE GET TO THEIR TRENCH...
MAYBE HE'S THE ONE WHO GOT GERMAIN AND SAUVEL LAST NIGHT.
WHY? YOU DON'T THINK THEY JUST DESERTED LIKE THE OTHERS?
MMM. IT'S ALMOST IMPOSSIBLE TO PASS THROUGH THE TRAPS AND LANDMINES WE PUT DOWN OUT THERE... ESPECIALLY AT NIGHT.
COULD BE. THOSE DAMN NIGHTS...

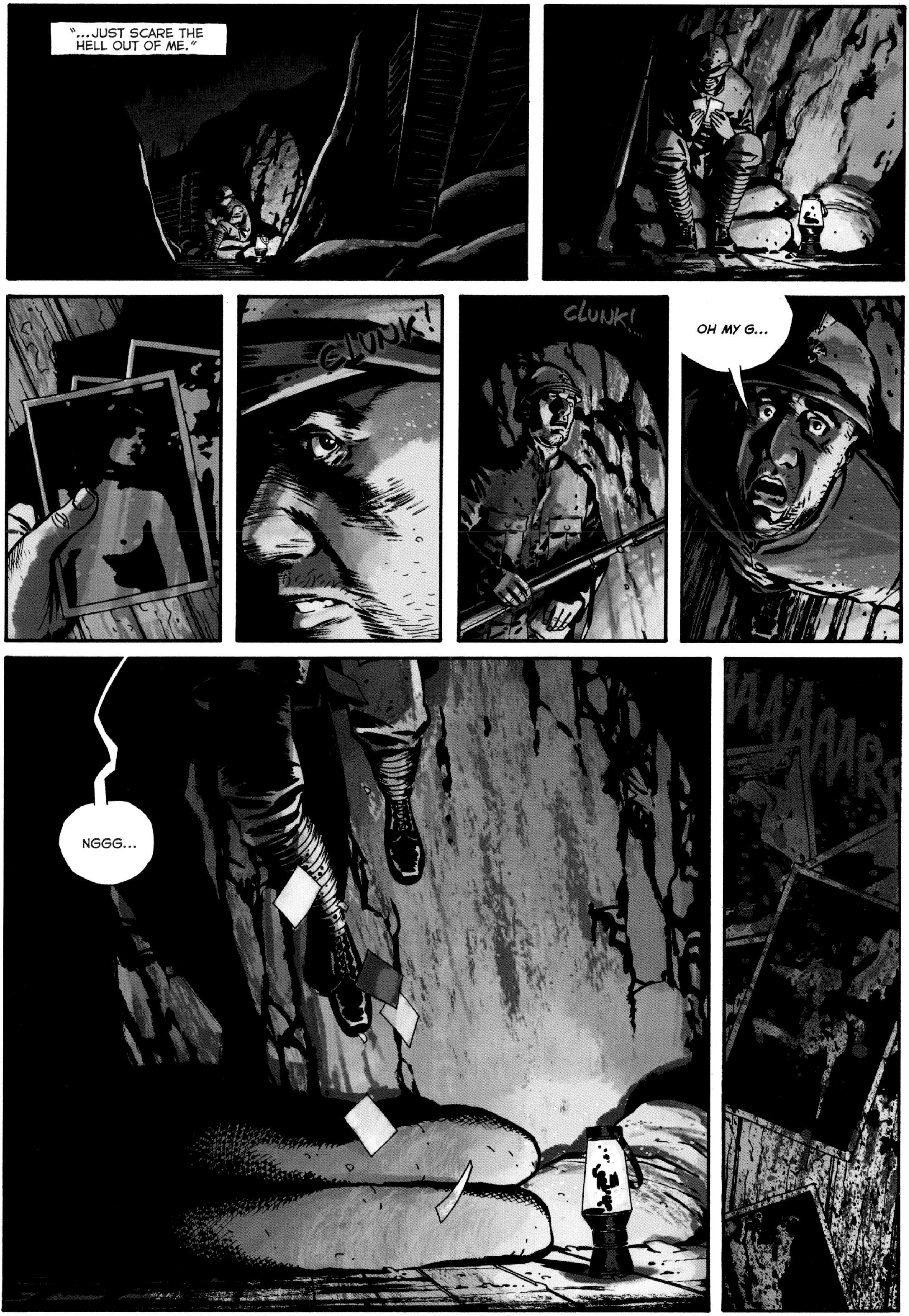
"...JUST SCARE THE HELL OUT OF ME."
CLUNK!
CLUNK!...
OH MY G...
NGGG...

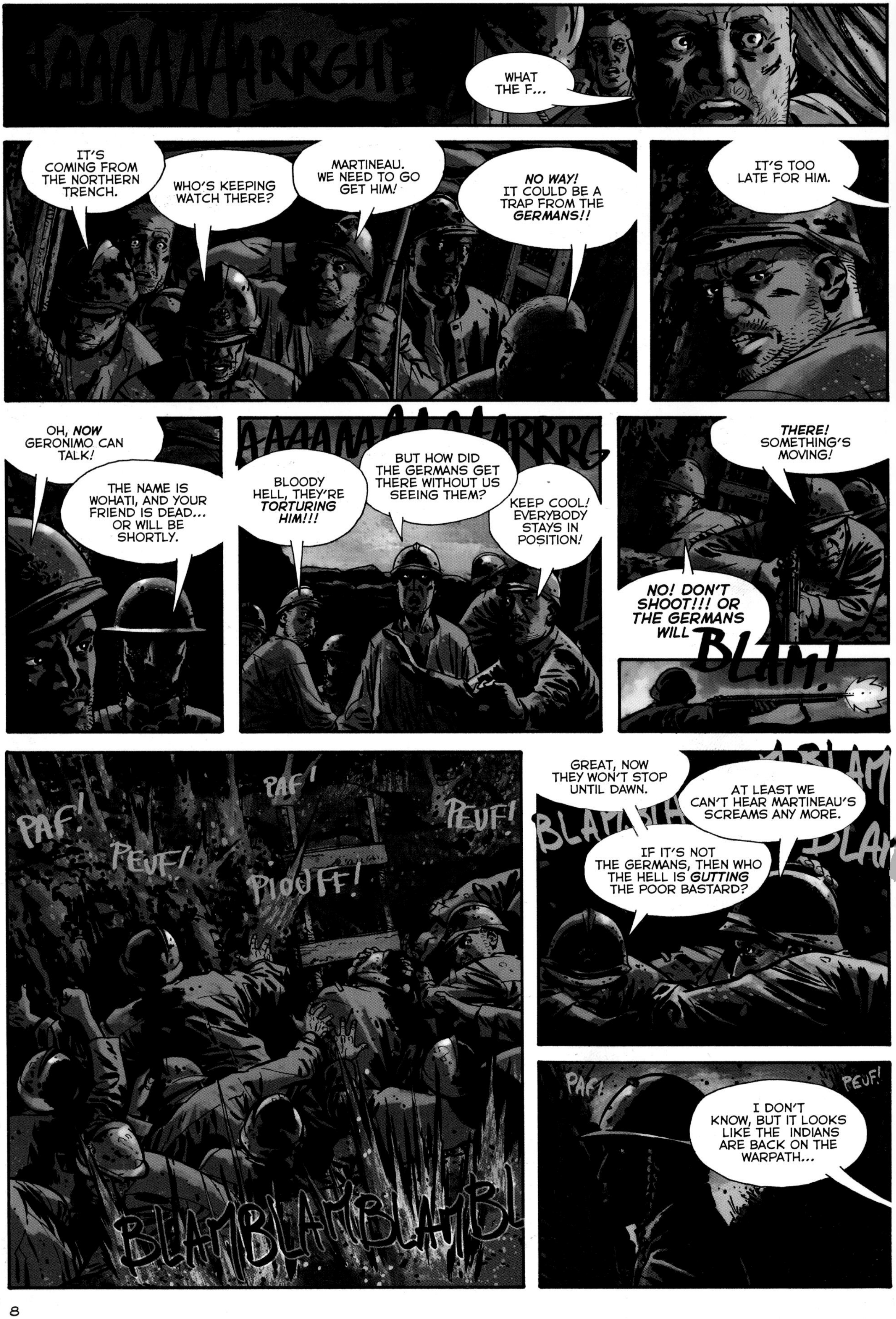
AAAAAAARRRGH!
WHAT THE F...
IT'S COMING FROM THE NORTHERN TRENCH.
WHO'S KEEPING WATCH THERE?
MARTINEAU. WE NEED TO GO GET HIM!
NO WAY! IT COULD BE A TRAP FROM THE GERMANS!!
IT'S TOO LATE FOR HIM.
OH, NOW GERONIMO CAN TALK!
THE NAME IS WOHATI, AND YOUR FRIEND IS DEAD... OR WILL BE SHORTLY.
AAAAAAAAAAARRRG
BLOODY HELL, THEY'RE TORTURING HIM!!!
BUT HOW DID THE GERMANS GET THERE WITHOUT US SEEING THEM?
KEEP COOL! EVERYBODY STAYS IN POSITION!
THERE! SOMETHING'S MOVING!
NO! DON'T SHOOT!!! OR THE GERMANS WILL
BLAM!
PAF!
PAF!
PEUF!
PEUF!
PIOUFF!
BLAMBLAMBLAMBL
GREAT, NOW THEY WON'T STOP UNTIL DAWN.
AT LEAST WE CAN'T HEAR MARTINEAU'S SCREAMS ANY MORE.
IF IT'S NOT THE GERMANS, THEN WHO THE HELL IS GUTTING THE POOR BASTARD?
PAF!
PEUF!
I DON'T KNOW, BUT IT LOOKS LIKE THE INDIANS ARE BACK ON THE WARPATH...

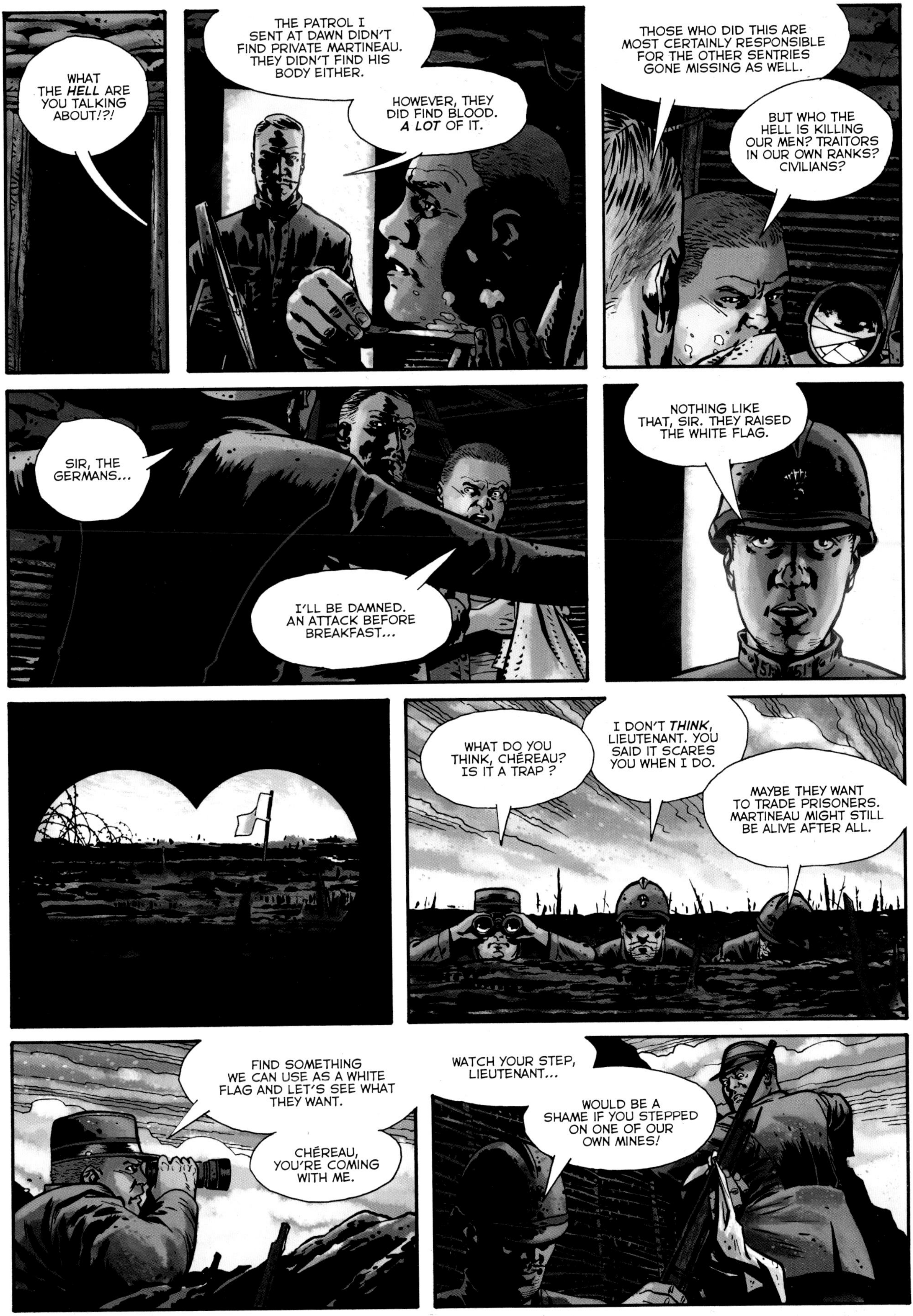
WHAT THE HELL ARE YOU TALKING ABOUT!?!
THE PATROL I SENT AT DAWN DIDN'T FIND PRIVATE MARTINEAU. THEY DIDN'T FIND HIS BODY EITHER.
HOWEVER, THEY DID FIND BLOOD. A LOT OF IT.
THOSE WHO DID THIS ARE MOST CERTAINLY RESPONSIBLE FOR THE OTHER SENTRIES GONE MISSING AS WELL.
BUT WHO THE HELL IS KILLING OUR MEN? TRAITORS IN OUR OWN RANKS? CIVILIANS?
SIR, THE GERMANS...
I'LL BE DAMNED. AN ATTACK BEFORE BREAKFAST...
NOTHING LIKE THAT, SIR. THEY RAISED THE WHITE FLAG.
WHAT DO YOU THINK, CHÉREAU? IS IT A TRAP ?
I DON'T THINK, LIEUTENANT. YOU SAID IT SCARES YOU WHEN I DO.
MAYBE THEY WANT TO TRADE PRISONERS. MARTINEAU MIGHT STILL BE ALIVE AFTER ALL.
FIND SOMETHING WE CAN USE AS A WHITE FLAG AND LET'S SEE WHAT THEY WANT.
CHÉREAU, YOU'RE COMING WITH ME.
WATCH YOUR STEP, LIEUTENANT...
WOULD BE A SHAME IF YOU STEPPED ON ONE OF OUR OWN MINES!

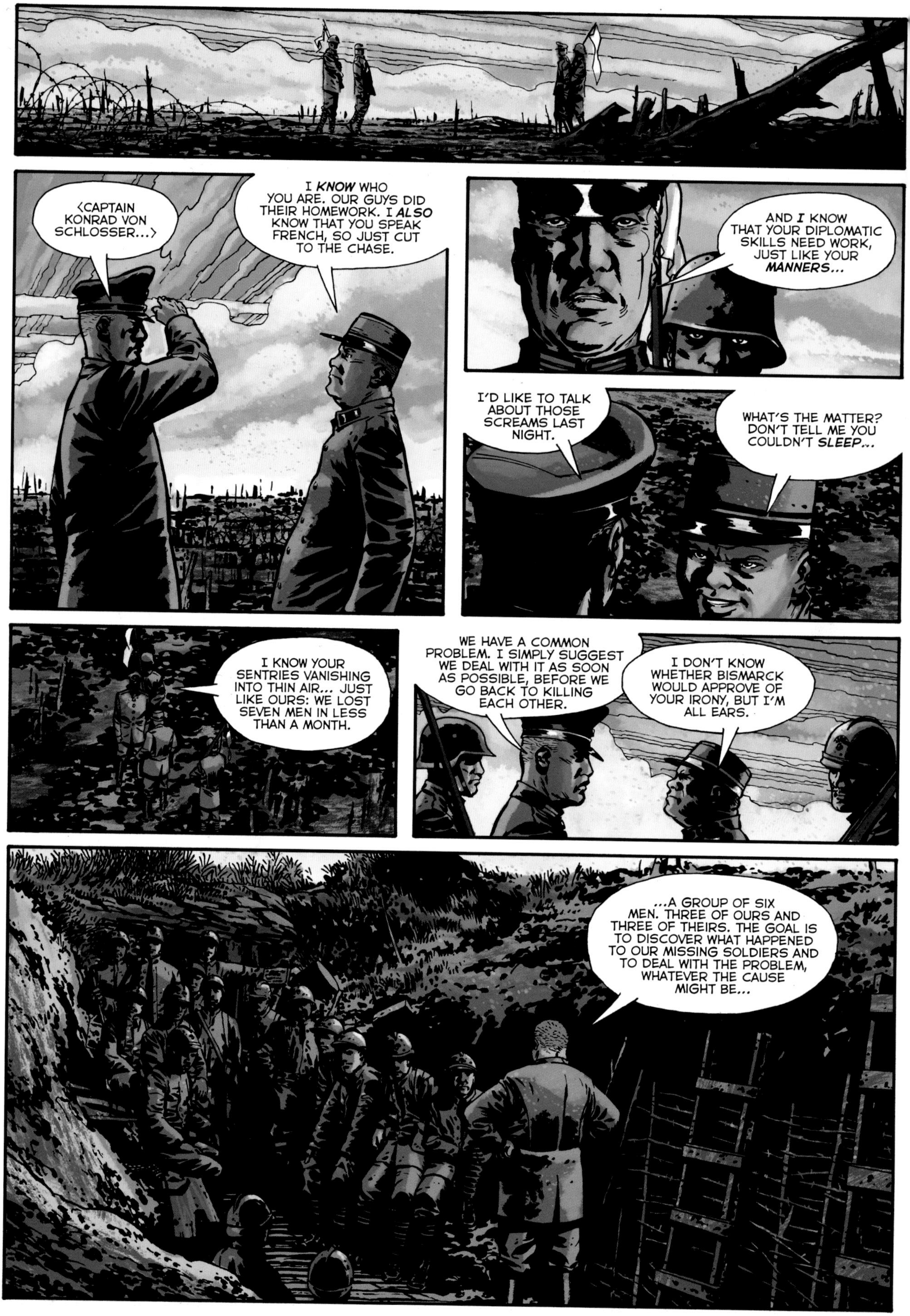

<CAPTAIN KONRAD VON SCHLOSSER...>
I KNOW WHO YOU ARE. OUR GUYS DID THEIR HOMEWORK. I ALSO KNOW THAT YOU SPEAK FRENCH, SO JUST CUT TO THE CHASE.
AND I KNOW THAT YOUR DIPLOMATIC SKILLS NEED WORK, JUST LIKE YOUR MANNERS...
I'D LIKE TO TALK ABOUT THOSE SCREAMS LAST NIGHT.
WHAT'S THE MATTER? DON'T TELL ME YOU COULDN'T SLEEP...
I KNOW YOUR SENTRIES VANISHING INTO THIN AIR... JUST LIKE OURS: WE LOST SEVEN MEN IN LESS THAN A MONTH.
WE HAVE A COMMON PROBLEM. I SIMPLY SUGGEST WE DEAL WITH IT AS SOON AS POSSIBLE, BEFORE WE GO BACK TO KILLING EACH OTHER.
I DON'T KNOW WHETHER BISMARCK WOULD APPROVE OF YOUR IRONY, BUT I'M ALL EARS.
...A GROUP OF SIX MEN. THREE OF OURS AND THREE OF THEIRS. THE GOAL IS TO DISCOVER WHAT HAPPENED TO OUR MISSING SOLDIERS AND TO DEAL WITH THE PROBLEM, WHATEVER THE CAUSE MIGHT BE...

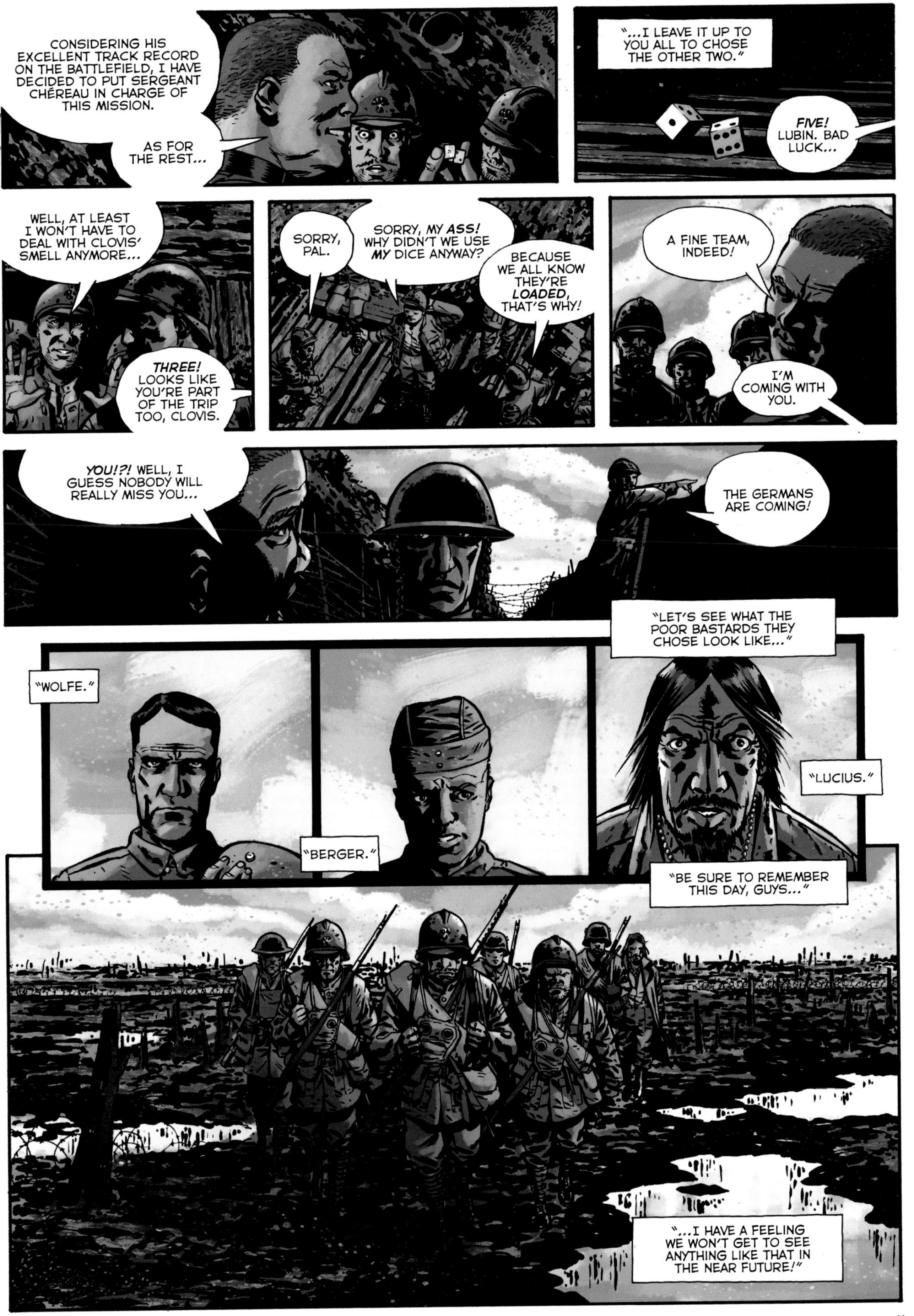

CONSIDERING HIS EXCELLENT TRACK RECORD ON THE BATTLEFIELD, I HAVE DECIDED TO PUT SERGEANT CHÉREAU IN CHARGE OF THIS MISSION.
AS FOR THE REST...
"...I LEAVE IT UP TO YOU ALL TO CHOSE THE OTHER TWO."
FIVE! LUBIN. BAD LUCK...
WELL, AT LEAST I WON'T HAVE TO DEAL WITH CLOVIS' SMELL ANYMORE...
THREE! LOOKS LIKE YOU'RE PART OF THE TRIP TOO, CLOVIS.
SORRY, PAL.
SORRY, MY ASS! WHY DIDN'T WE USE MY DICE ANYWAY?
BECAUSE WE ALL KNOW THEY'RE LOADED, THAT'S WHY!
A FINE TEAM, INDEED!
I'M COMING WITH YOU.
YOU!?! WELL, I GUESS NOBODY WILL REALLY MISS YOU...
THE GERMANS ARE COMING!
"LET'S SEE WHAT THE POOR BASTARDS THEY CHOSE LOOK LIKE..."
"WOLFE."
"BERGER."
"LUCIUS."
"BE SURE TO REMEMBER THIS DAY, GUYS..."
"...I HAVE A FEELING WE WON'T GET TO SEE ANYTHING LIKE THAT IN THE NEAR FUTURE!"

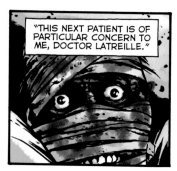

"THIS NEXT PATIENT IS OF PARTICULAR CONCERN TO ME, DOCTOR LATREILLE."

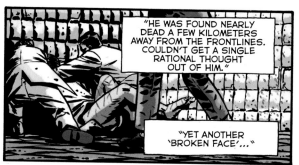

"HE WAS FOUND NEARLY DEAD A FEW KILOMETERS AWAY FROM THE FRONTLINES. COULDN'T GET A SINGLE RATIONAL THOUGHT OUT OF HIM."

"YET ANOTHER 'BROKEN FACE'..."

"THAT IS INDEED WHAT WE THOUGHT AT THE BEGINNING."

"HIS ERRATIC BEHAVIOUR IS CONSISTENT WITH WHAT HAS BEEN OBSERVED ON OTHER SHELL-SHOCKED PATIENTS."

CONSIDERING THE SERIOUSNESS OF HIS WOUNDS, I AM NOT SURPRISED HE IS SHOWING SIGNS OF DISSOCIATIVE DISORDER...

AND YET I HAVE A HARD TIME BELIEVING THAT SHRAPNEL COULD HAVE CAUSED SUCH DAMAGE WITHOUT *KILLING* HIM...

YOU KNOW WHAT TO DO NEXT, FAURE. OBVIOUSLY YOU NEED TO KNOW MORE ABOUT YOUR PATIENT'S WHEREABOUTS IF YOU MEAN TO TREAT HIM.

NO *FACE*. NO *NAME*. WE'RE STILL TRYING TO FIND OUT MORE ABOUT HIS RECENT POSTING...

"AND THEN HE HAS THOSE HORRIBLE MARKS ALL OVER HIS BODY..."

"I COULD SWEAR THEY'RE *BITE* MARKS."

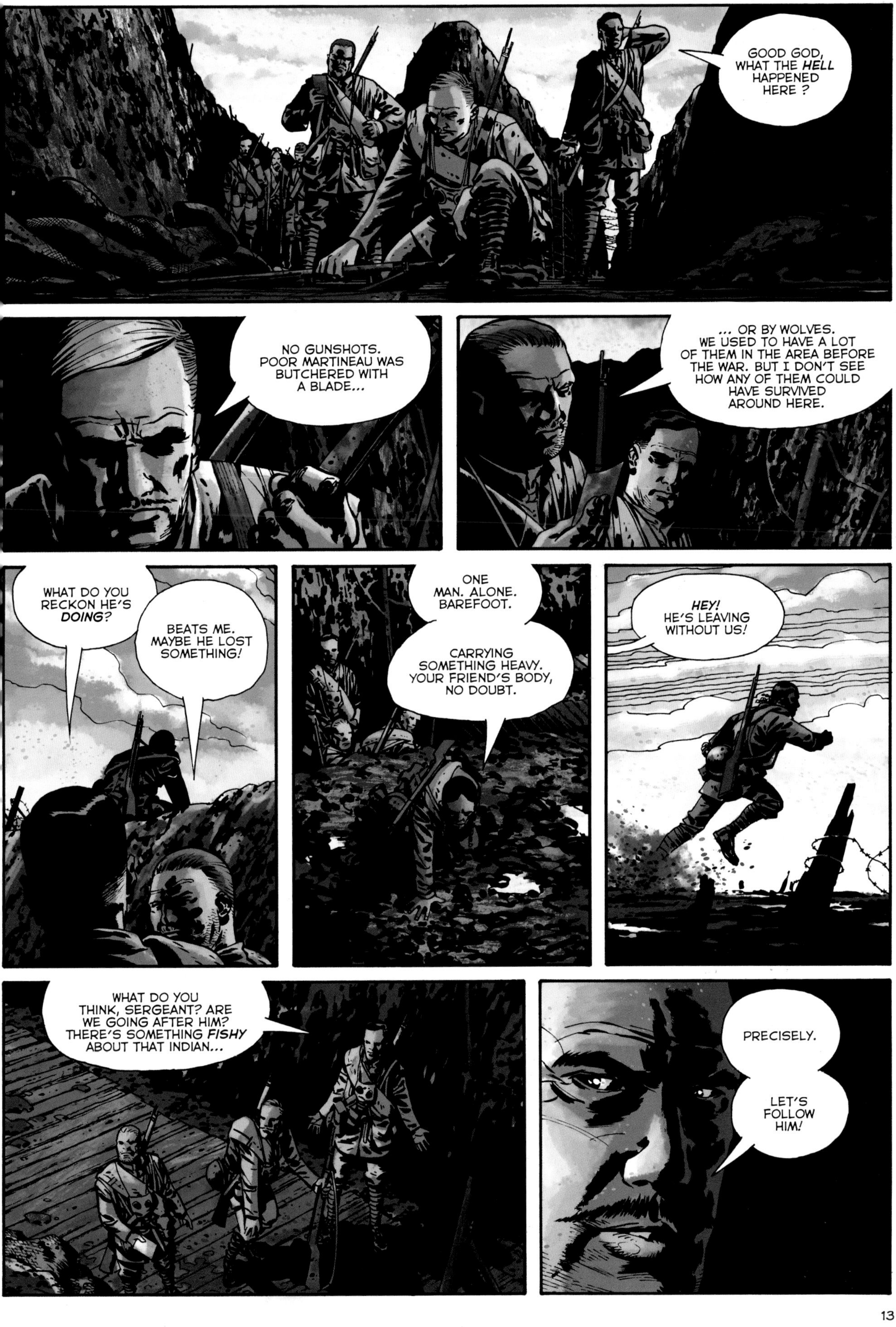
GOOD GOD, WHAT THE HELL HAPPENED HERE ?
NO GUNSHOTS. POOR MARTINEAU WAS BUTCHERED WITH A BLADE...
... OR BY WOLVES. WE USED TO HAVE A LOT OF THEM IN THE AREA BEFORE THE WAR. BUT I DON'T SEE HOW ANY OF THEM COULD HAVE SURVIVED AROUND HERE.
WHAT DO YOU RECKON HE'S DOING?
BEATS ME. MAYBE HE LOST SOMETHING!
ONE MAN. ALONE. BAREFOOT.
CARRYING SOMETHING HEAVY. YOUR FRIEND'S BODY, NO DOUBT.
HEY! HE'S LEAVING WITHOUT US!
WHAT DO YOU THINK, SERGEANT? ARE WE GOING AFTER HIM? THERE'S SOMETHING FISHY ABOUT THAT INDIAN...
PRECISELY.
LET'S FOLLOW HIM!

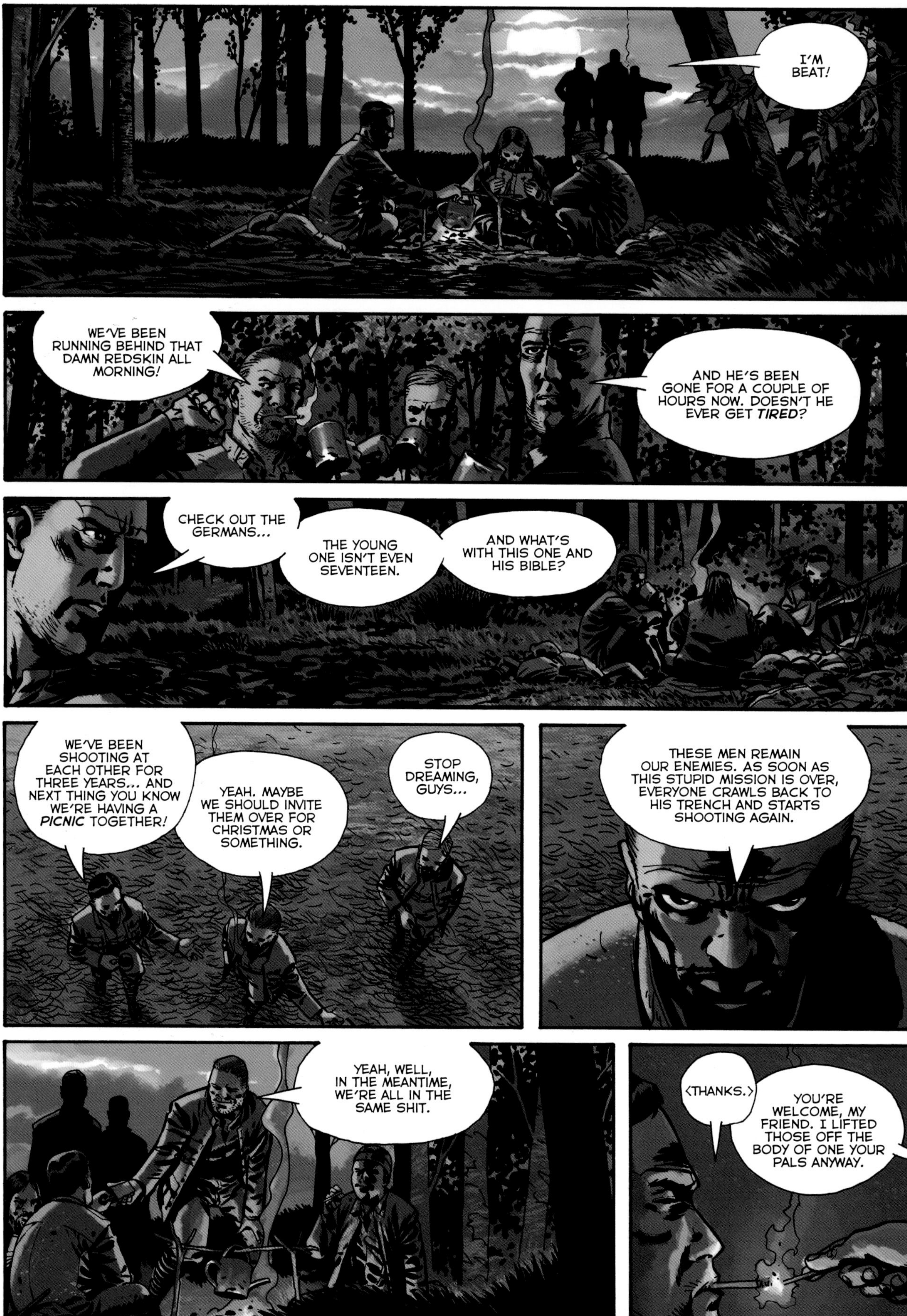
I'M BEAT!
WE'VE BEEN RUNNING BEHIND THAT DAMN REDSKIN ALL MORNING!
AND HE'S BEEN GONE FOR A COUPLE OF HOURS NOW. DOESN'T HE EVER GET TIRED?
CHECK OUT THE GERMANS...
THE YOUNG ONE ISN'T EVEN SEVENTEEN.
AND WHAT'S WITH THIS ONE AND HIS BIBLE?
WE'VE BEEN SHOOTING AT EACH OTHER FOR THREE YEARS... AND NEXT THING YOU KNOW WE'RE HAVING A PICNIC TOGETHER!
YEAH. MAYBE WE SHOULD INVITE THEM OVER FOR CHRISTMAS OR SOMETHING.
STOP DREAMING, GUYS...
THESE MEN REMAIN OUR ENEMIES. AS SOON AS THIS STUPID MISSION IS OVER, EVERYONE CRAWLS BACK TO HIS TRENCH AND STARTS SHOOTING AGAIN.
YEAH, WELL, IN THE MEANTIME, WE'RE ALL IN THE SAME SHIT.
<THANKS.>
YOU'RE WELCOME, MY FRIEND. I LIFTED THOSE OFF THE BODY OF ONE YOUR PALS ANYWAY.

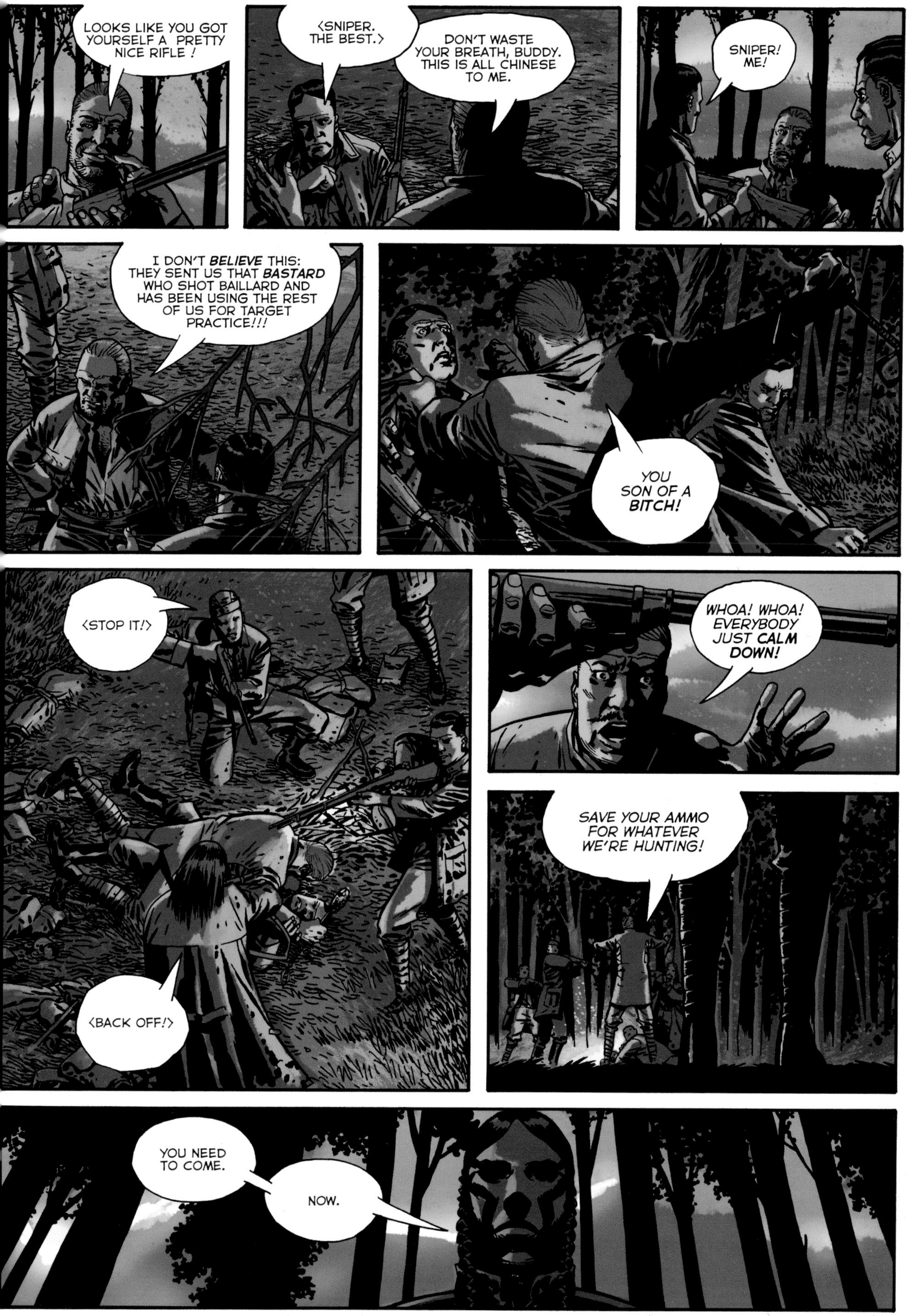
LOOKS LIKE YOU GOT YOURSELF A PRETTY NICE RIFLE !
<SNIPER. THE BEST.>
DON'T WASTE YOUR BREATH, BUDDY. THIS IS ALL CHINESE TO ME.
SNIPER! ME!
I DON'T BELIEVE THIS: THEY SENT US THAT BASTARD WHO SHOT BAILLARD AND HAS BEEN USING THE REST OF US FOR TARGET PRACTICE!!!
YOU SON OF A BITCH!
<STOP IT!>
<BACK OFF!>
WHOA! WHOA! EVERYBODY JUST CALM DOWN!
SAVE YOUR AMMO FOR WHATEVER WE'RE HUNTING!
YOU NEED TO COME.
NOW.

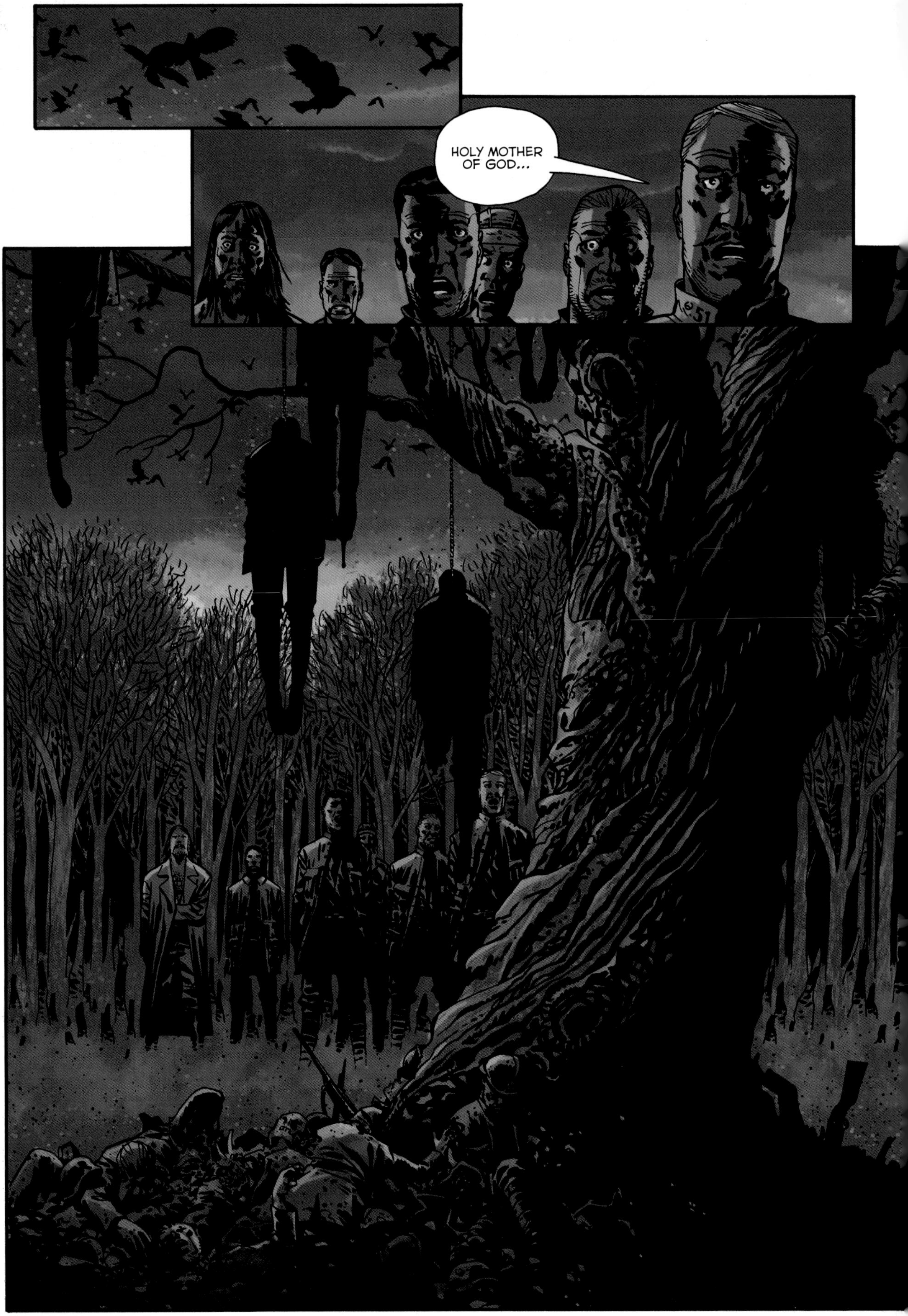
HOLY MOTHER OF GOD...

DESERTERS, *MY ASS!* AND WE ALL THOUGHT THEY WERE JUST *RELAXING* SOMEPLACE SAFE...

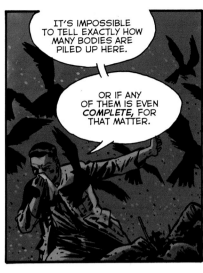

IT'S IMPOSSIBLE TO TELL EXACTLY HOW MANY BODIES ARE PILED UP HERE.

OR IF ANY OF THEM IS EVEN *COMPLETE,* FOR THAT MATTER.

⟨THE DEVIL!⟩

THE DEVIL? I DON'T THINK SO. EVEN *HE* DOESN'T HAVE THAT KIND OF TWISTED IMAGINATION.

IN ANY CASE, I'VE NEVER SEEN ANYTHING LIKE THIS.

I HAVE: IN MY UNCLE'S BUTCHER SHOP BEFORE THE WAR. THESE GUYS UP THERE WERE SKINNED AND CUT UP LIKE THEY WERE JUST... MEAT.

LOOKS LIKE WE JUST FOUND SOMEBODY'S FOOD SUPPLY.

YOU THINK...

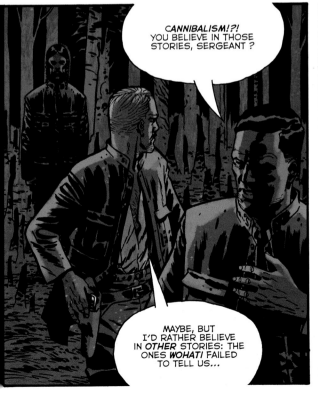

CANNIBALISM!?! YOU BELIEVE IN THOSE STORIES, SERGEANT?

MAYBE, BUT I'D RATHER BELIEVE IN *OTHER* STORIES: THE ONES *WOHALI* FAILED TO TELL US...

...AND I WANT TO HEAR THOSE STORIES *RIGHT NOW,* INDIAN!

THERE'S ONLY ONE STORY TO TELL.

THAT OF THE *WENDIGO.*

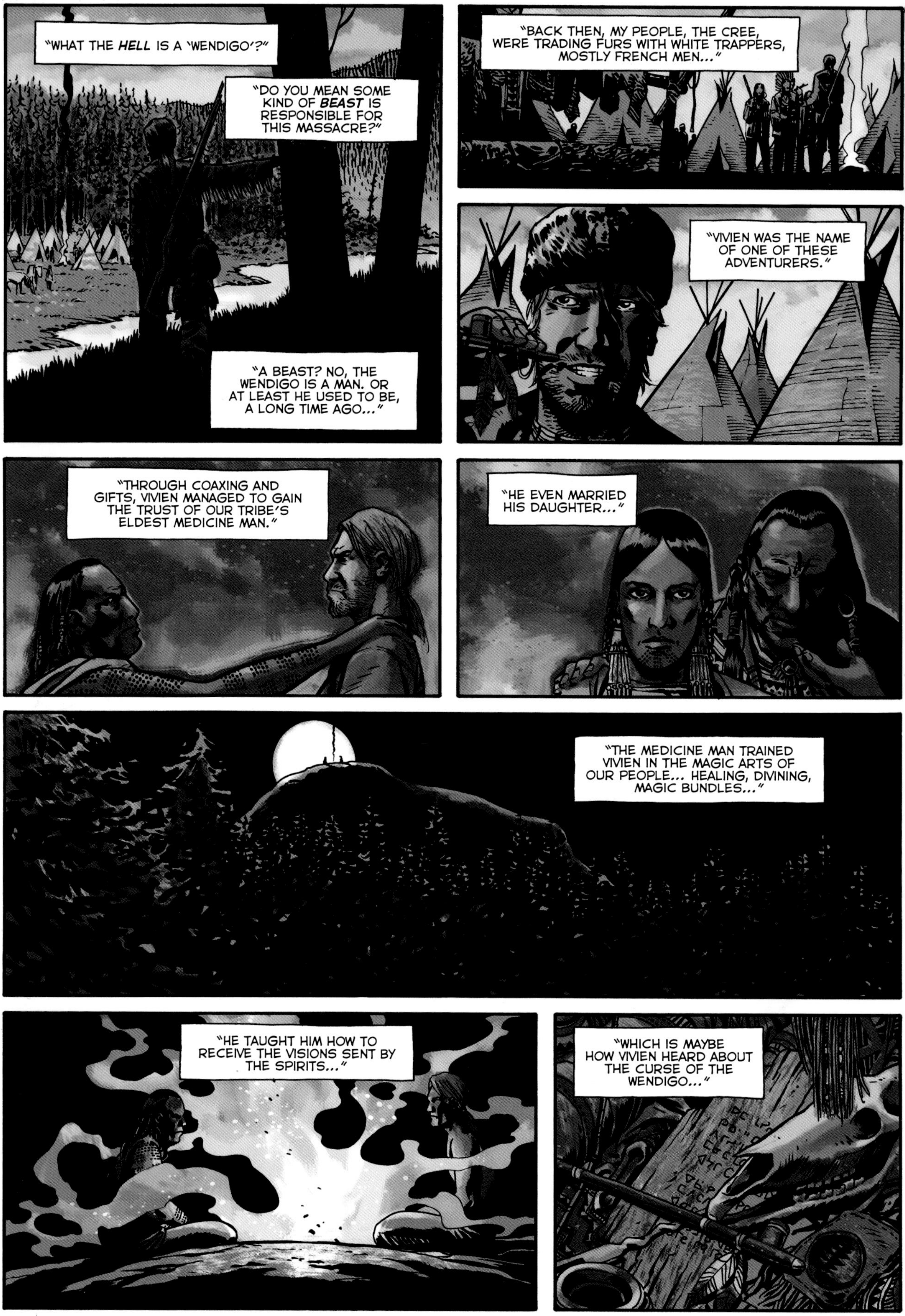
"WHAT THE HELL IS A 'WENDIGO'?"
"DO YOU MEAN SOME KIND OF BEAST IS RESPONSIBLE FOR THIS MASSACRE?"
"A BEAST? NO, THE WENDIGO IS A MAN. OR AT LEAST HE USED TO BE, A LONG TIME AGO..."
"BACK THEN, MY PEOPLE, THE CREE, WERE TRADING FURS WITH WHITE TRAPPERS, MOSTLY FRENCH MEN..."
"VIVIEN WAS THE NAME OF ONE OF THESE ADVENTURERS."
"THROUGH COAXING AND GIFTS, VIVIEN MANAGED TO GAIN THE TRUST OF OUR TRIBE'S ELDEST MEDICINE MAN."
"HE EVEN MARRIED HIS DAUGHTER..."
"THE MEDICINE MAN TRAINED VIVIEN IN THE MAGIC ARTS OF OUR PEOPLE... HEALING, DIVINING, MAGIC BUNDLES..."
"HE TAUGHT HIM HOW TO RECEIVE THE VISIONS SENT BY THE SPIRITS..."
"WHICH IS MAYBE HOW VIVIEN HEARD ABOUT THE CURSE OF THE WENDIGO..."

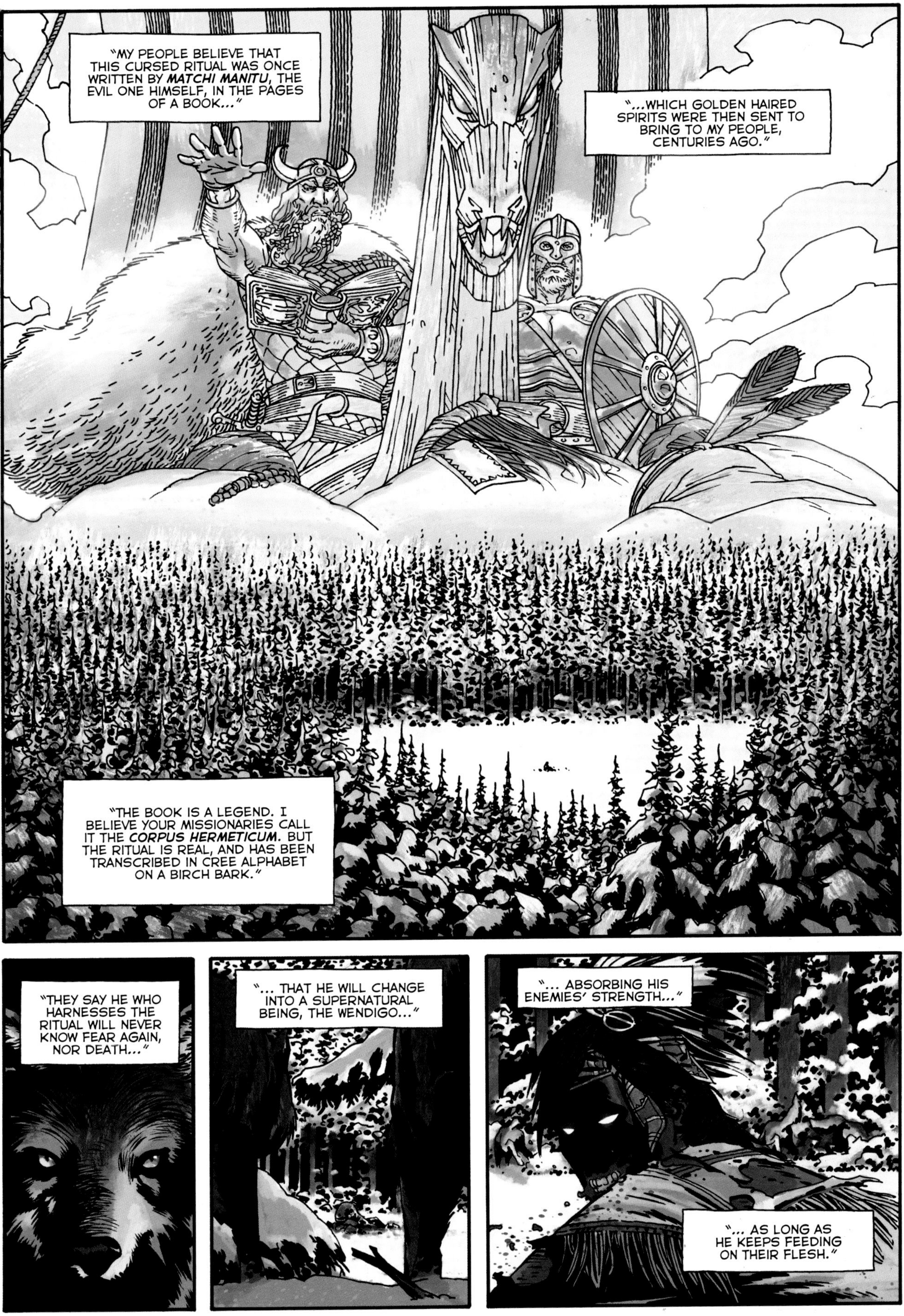
"MY PEOPLE BELIEVE THAT THIS CURSED RITUAL WAS ONCE WRITTEN BY MATCHI MANITU, THE EVIL ONE HIMSELF, IN THE PAGES OF A BOOK..."
"...WHICH GOLDEN HAIRED SPIRITS WERE THEN SENT TO BRING TO MY PEOPLE, CENTURIES AGO."
"THE BOOK IS A LEGEND. I BELIEVE YOUR MISSIONARIES CALL IT THE CORPUS HERMETICUM. BUT THE RITUAL IS REAL, AND HAS BEEN TRANSCRIBED IN CREE ALPHABET ON A BIRCH BARK."
"THEY SAY HE WHO HARNESSES THE RITUAL WILL NEVER KNOW FEAR AGAIN, NOR DEATH..."
"... THAT HE WILL CHANGE INTO A SUPERNATURAL BEING, THE WENDIGO..."
"... ABSORBING HIS ENEMIES' STRENGTH..."
"... AS LONG AS HE KEEPS FEEDING ON THEIR FLESH."

"LURED BY THE PROMISE OF SUCH POWER, VIVIEN STOLE THE RITUAL DURING THE NIGHT."

"NOTHING COULD STOP HIM NOW."

"HE WAS READY TO PAY THE PRICE."

"VIVIEN LEFT THE CAMP THAT SAME NIGHT..."

"... LEAVING ONLY PAIN AND GRIEF BEHIND HIM."

"IT TOOK ANOTHER HUNDRED YEARS BEFORE KICE MANITU, THE CREATOR OF ALL THINGS, TRUSTED SOMEONE WITH THE TASK OF SEEKING REVENGE FOR THE OFFENSE MADE TO MY TRIBE."

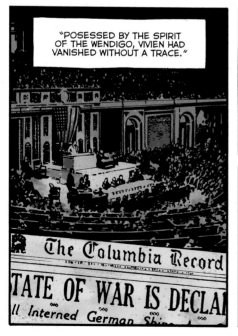

"POSESSED BY THE SPIRIT OF THE WENDIGO, VIVIEN HAD VANISHED WITHOUT A TRACE."

The Columbia Record

TATE OF WAR IS DECLA

ll Interned German Ship

"BUT THE GREAT MANITU GUIDED EVERY SINGLE ONE OF MY STEPS..."

"I HAVE CROSSED LAND AND SEA ON THE TRAIL OF THE MONSTER..."

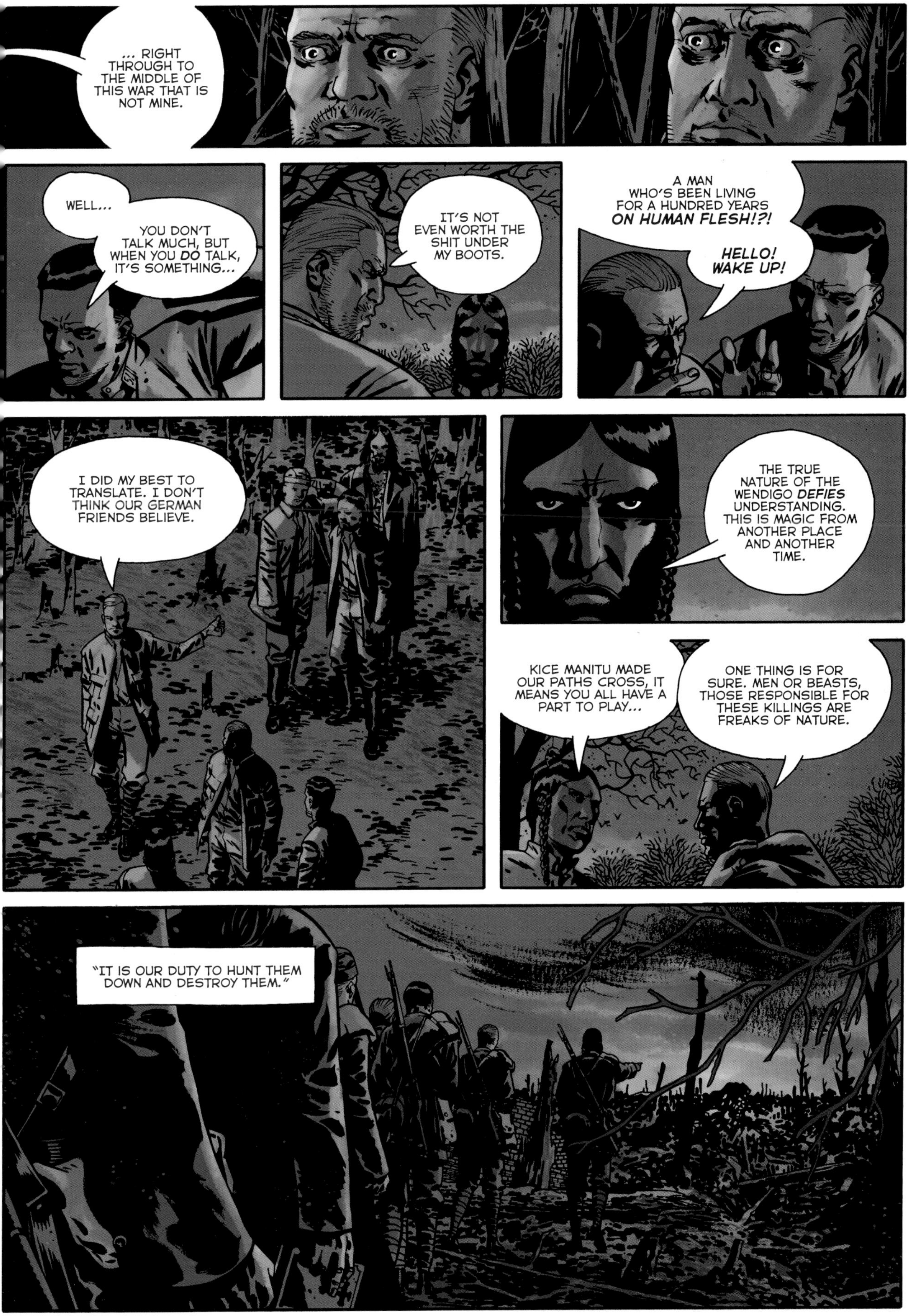
... RIGHT THROUGH TO THE MIDDLE OF THIS WAR THAT IS NOT MINE.
WELL...
YOU DON'T TALK MUCH, BUT WHEN YOU *DO* TALK, IT'S SOMETHING...
IT'S NOT EVEN WORTH THE SHIT UNDER MY BOOTS.
A MAN WHO'S BEEN LIVING FOR A HUNDRED YEARS ***ON HUMAN FLESH!?!***
HELLO! WAKE UP!
I DID MY BEST TO TRANSLATE. I DON'T THINK OUR GERMAN FRIENDS BELIEVE.
THE TRUE NATURE OF THE WENDIGO ***DEFIES*** UNDERSTANDING. THIS IS MAGIC FROM ANOTHER PLACE AND ANOTHER TIME.
KICE MANITU MADE OUR PATHS CROSS, IT MEANS YOU ALL HAVE A PART TO PLAY...
ONE THING IS FOR SURE. MEN OR BEASTS, THOSE RESPONSIBLE FOR THESE KILLINGS ARE FREAKS OF NATURE.
"IT IS OUR DUTY TO HUNT THEM DOWN AND DESTROY THEM."

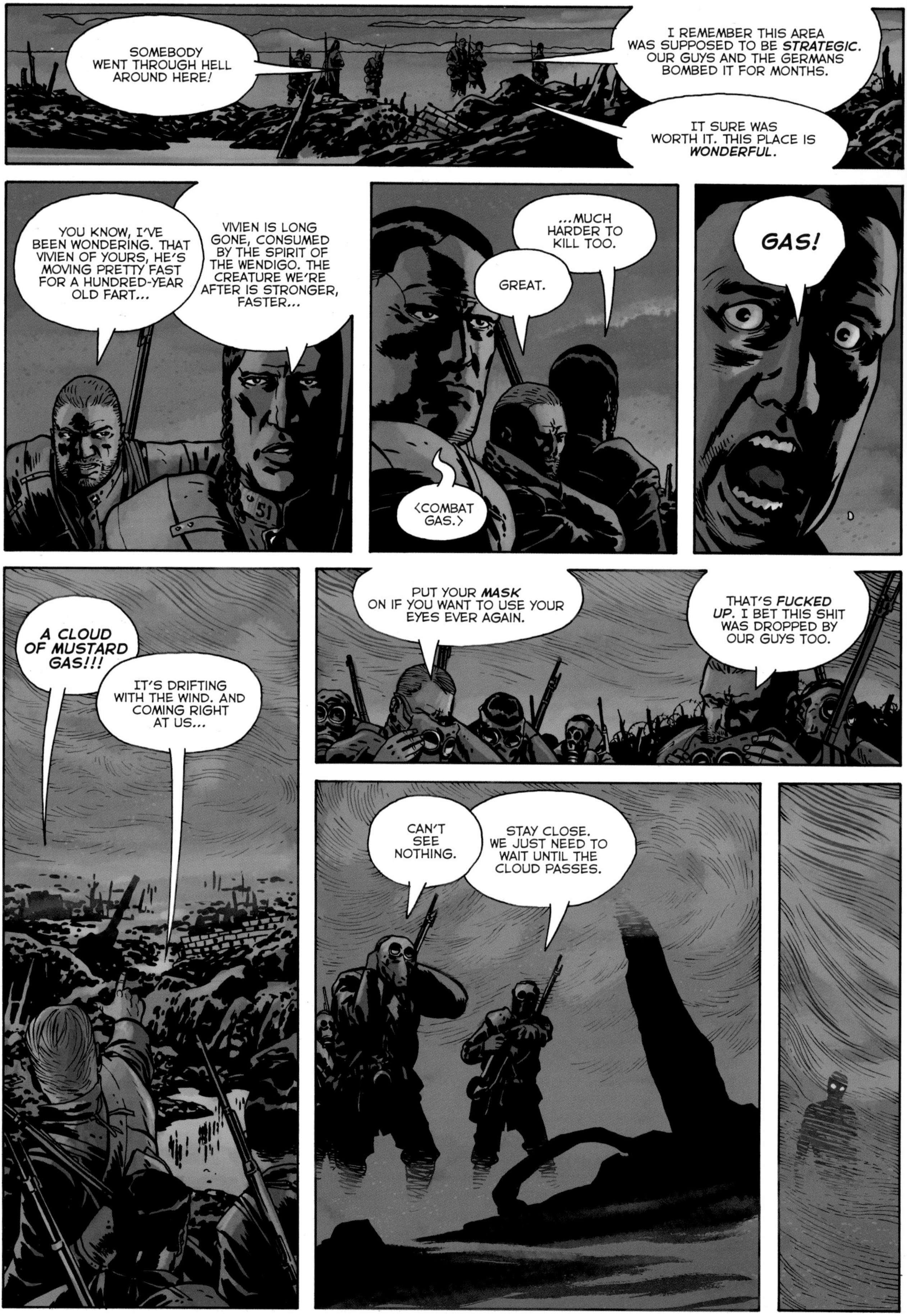
SOMEBODY WENT THROUGH HELL AROUND HERE!
I REMEMBER THIS AREA WAS SUPPOSED TO BE STRATEGIC. OUR GUYS AND THE GERMANS BOMBED IT FOR MONTHS.
IT SURE WAS WORTH IT. THIS PLACE IS WONDERFUL.
YOU KNOW, I'VE BEEN WONDERING. THAT VIVIEN OF YOURS, HE'S MOVING PRETTY FAST FOR A HUNDRED-YEAR OLD FART...
VIVIEN IS LONG GONE, CONSUMED BY THE SPIRIT OF THE WENDIGO. THE CREATURE WE'RE AFTER IS STRONGER, FASTER...
...MUCH HARDER TO KILL TOO.
GREAT.
<COMBAT GAS.>
GAS!
A CLOUD OF MUSTARD GAS!!!
IT'S DRIFTING WITH THE WIND. AND COMING RIGHT AT US...
PUT YOUR MASK ON IF YOU WANT TO USE YOUR EYES EVER AGAIN.
THAT'S FUCKED UP. I BET THIS SHIT WAS DROPPED BY OUR GUYS TOO.
CAN'T SEE NOTHING.
STAY CLOSE. WE JUST NEED TO WAIT UNTIL THE CLOUD PASSES.

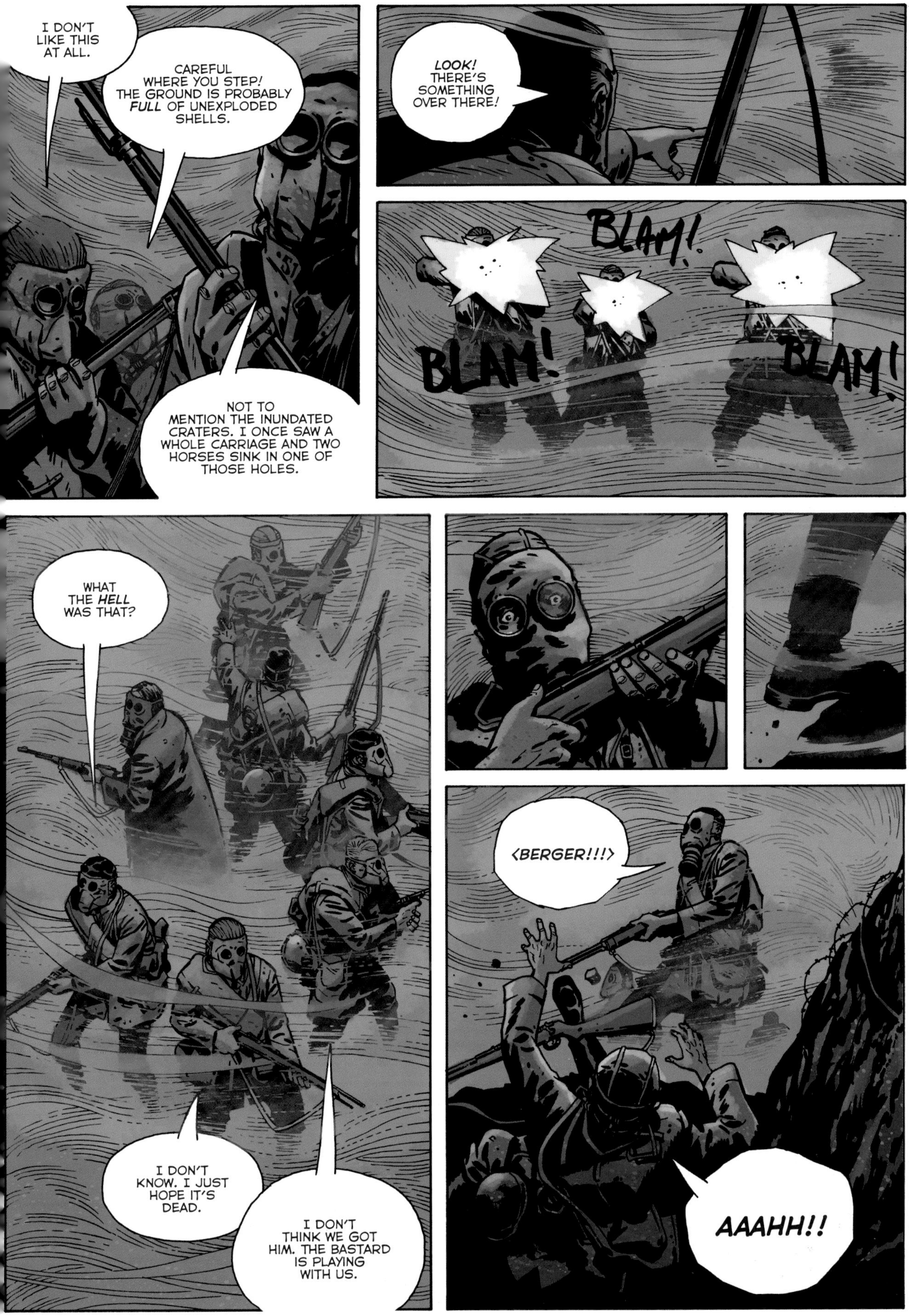
I DON'T LIKE THIS AT ALL.
CAREFUL WHERE YOU STEP! THE GROUND IS PROBABLY *FULL* OF UNEXPLODED SHELLS.
NOT TO MENTION THE INUNDATED CRATERS. I ONCE SAW A WHOLE CARRIAGE AND TWO HORSES SINK IN ONE OF THOSE HOLES.
LOOK! THERE'S SOMETHING OVER THERE!
BLAM!
BLAM!
BLAM!
WHAT THE *HELL* WAS THAT?
I DON'T KNOW. I JUST HOPE IT'S DEAD.
I DON'T THINK WE GOT HIM. THE BASTARD IS PLAYING WITH US.
<BERGER!!!>
AAAHH!!

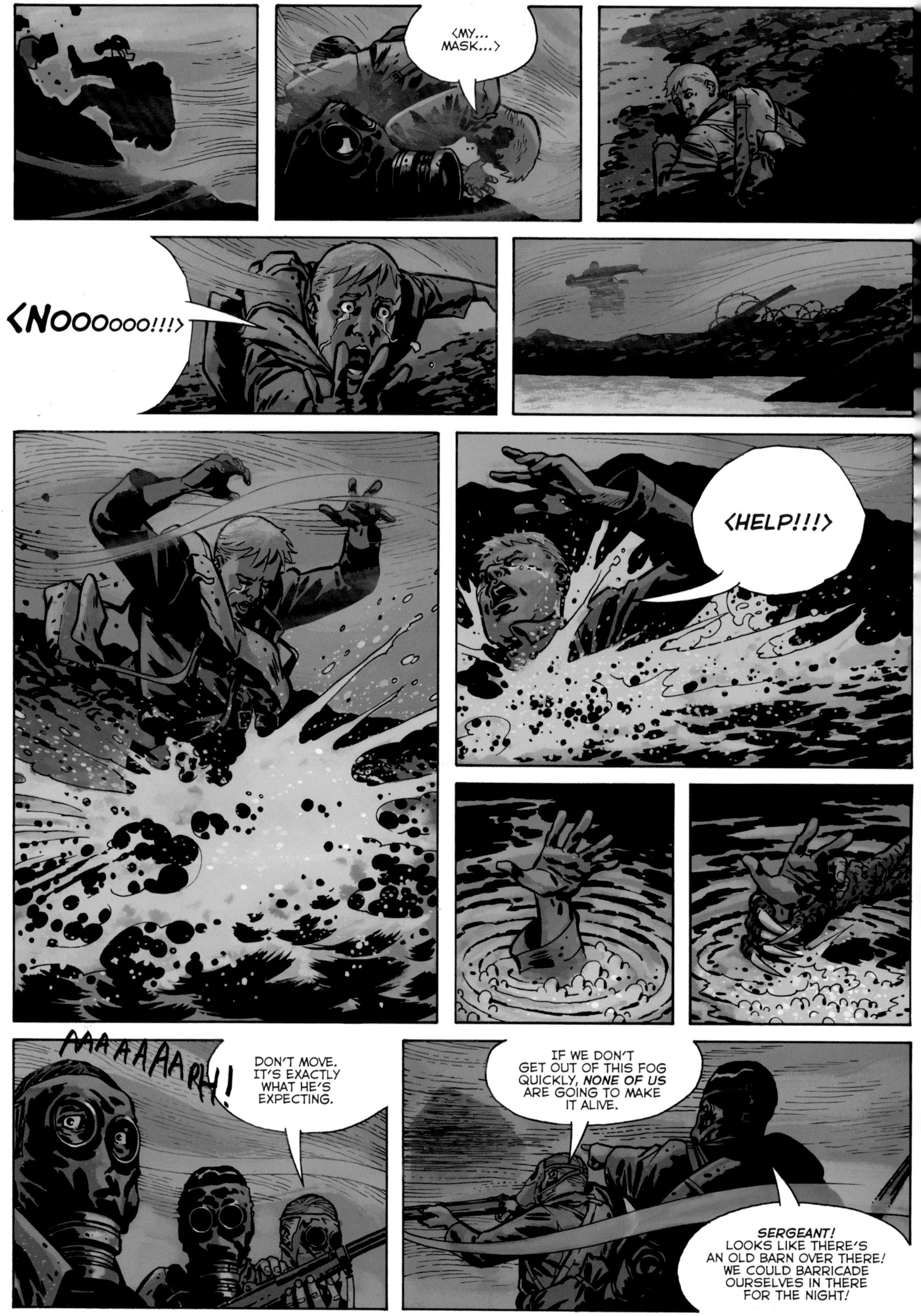
<MY... MASK...>
<NOOOOOO!!!>
<HELP!!!>
AAAAAAARH!
DON'T MOVE. IT'S EXACTLY WHAT HE'S EXPECTING.
IF WE DON'T GET OUT OF THIS FOG QUICKLY, NONE OF US ARE GOING TO MAKE IT ALIVE.
SERGEANT! LOOKS LIKE THERE'S AN OLD BARN OVER THERE! WE COULD BARRICADE OURSELVES IN THERE FOR THE NIGHT!

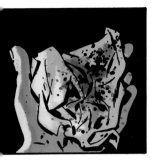

EVEN WITH OUR *MASKS* ON, THOSE CHEMICALS EAT US FROM THE INSIDE!

AT LEAST THE CLOUD MOVED ON...

SEE ANYTHING?

NO...

... BUT I KNOW HE'S OUT THERE, SOMWHERE.

YOU'RE SHAKING, LUBIN. ARE YOU AFRAID?

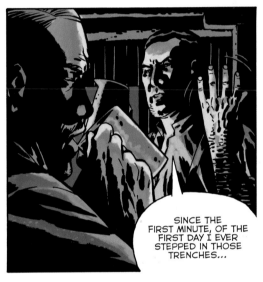

SINCE THE FIRST MINUTE, OF THE FIRST DAY I EVER STEPPED IN THOSE TRENCHES...

NOBODY CAN HOLD IT AGAINST YOU, LUBIN. YOU PROVED YOURSELF IN COMBAT.

I JUST PROVED THAT I WAS TOO SCARED TO THINK ABOUT ANYTHING BEYOND WALKING STRAIGHT TOWARDS GERMAN FIRE. *TWO YEARS* I'VE BEEN WAITING FOR THAT ONE SINGLE BULLET, SHOT BY A FRIEND OR A FOE, THAT WILL STOP THE FEAR...

WELL, I CAN'T SAY THIS IS THE KIND OF SPEECH MY HIERARCHY WOULD APPROVE...

I DON'T EXPECT YOU TO UNDERSTAND, SERGEANT. YOU ARE A PROFESSIONAL SOLDIER. YOU WERE *BORN* TO FIGHT THIS WAR.

ME, I USED TO BE A SALESMAN, IN A DEPARTMENT STORE. "LADIES FASHION" AISLE. I REMEMBER I USED TO GENTLY PINCH THE CLIENTS' THIGHS AS I WAS ADJUSTING THEIR DRESSES.

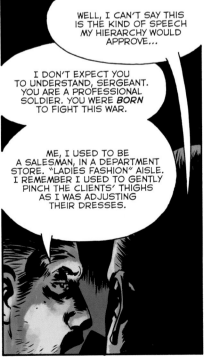

THE NEXT THING I KNOW, I'VE BEEN TRANSFERRED TO THE *BUTCHER SHOP*. I'M CRAWLING IN THE MUD TO RETRIEVE A FRIEND'S LEG, WHILE HE YELLS THAT HE WASN'T HIT AND HE IS PERFECTLY ALL RIGHT.

AND NOW... THIS.

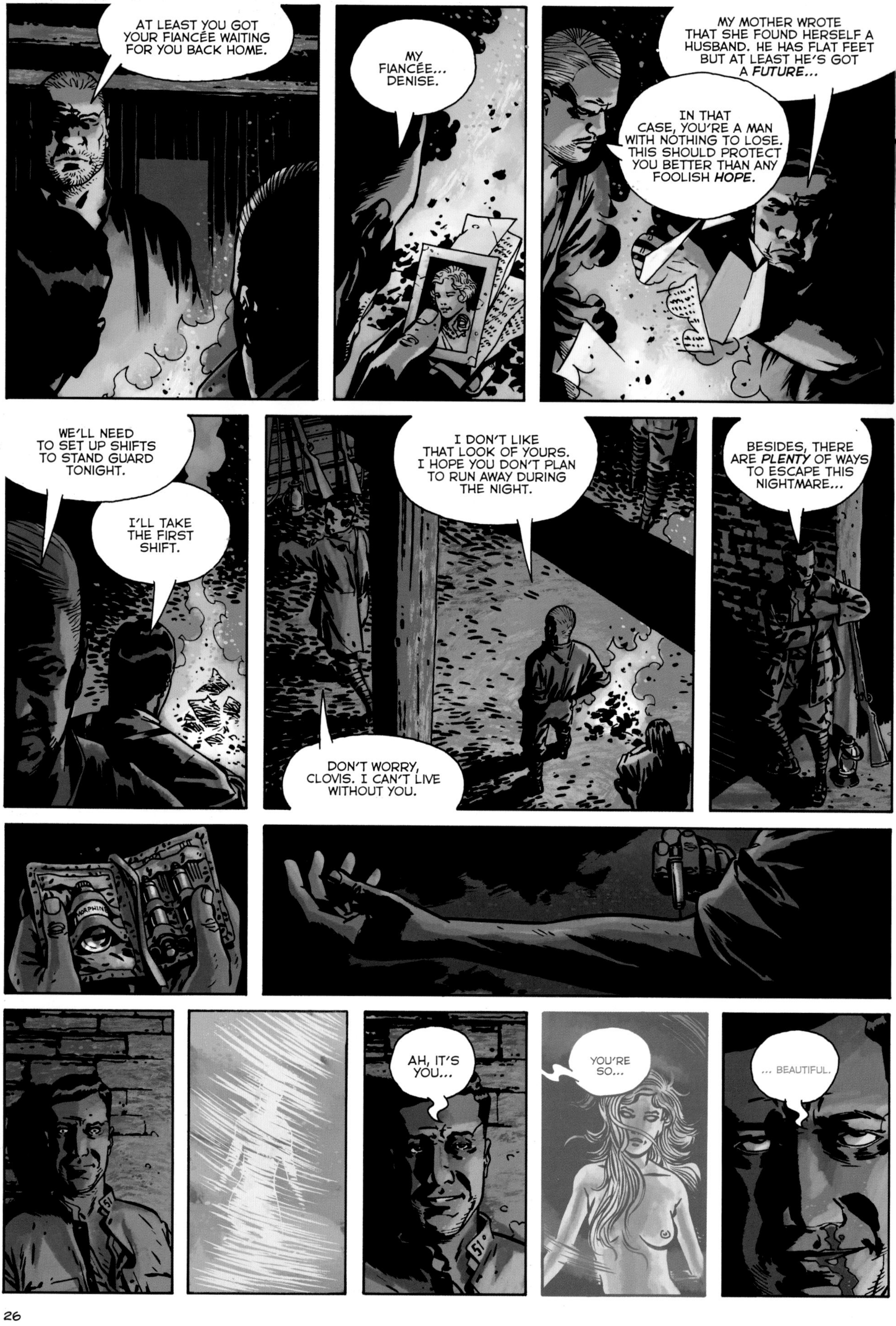
AT LEAST YOU GOT YOUR FIANCÉE WAITING FOR YOU BACK HOME.
MY FIANCÉE... DENISE.
MY MOTHER WROTE THAT SHE FOUND HERSELF A HUSBAND. HE HAS FLAT FEET BUT AT LEAST HE'S GOT A *FUTURE*...
IN THAT CASE, YOU'RE A MAN WITH NOTHING TO LOSE. THIS SHOULD PROTECT YOU BETTER THAN ANY FOOLISH *HOPE*.
WE'LL NEED TO SET UP SHIFTS TO STAND GUARD TONIGHT.
I'LL TAKE THE FIRST SHIFT.
I DON'T LIKE THAT LOOK OF YOURS. I HOPE YOU DON'T PLAN TO RUN AWAY DURING THE NIGHT.
DON'T WORRY, CLOVIS. I CAN'T LIVE WITHOUT YOU.
BESIDES, THERE ARE *PLENTY* OF WAYS TO ESCAPE THIS NIGHTMARE...
MORPHINE
AH, IT'S YOU...
YOU'RE SO...
... BEAUTIFUL.

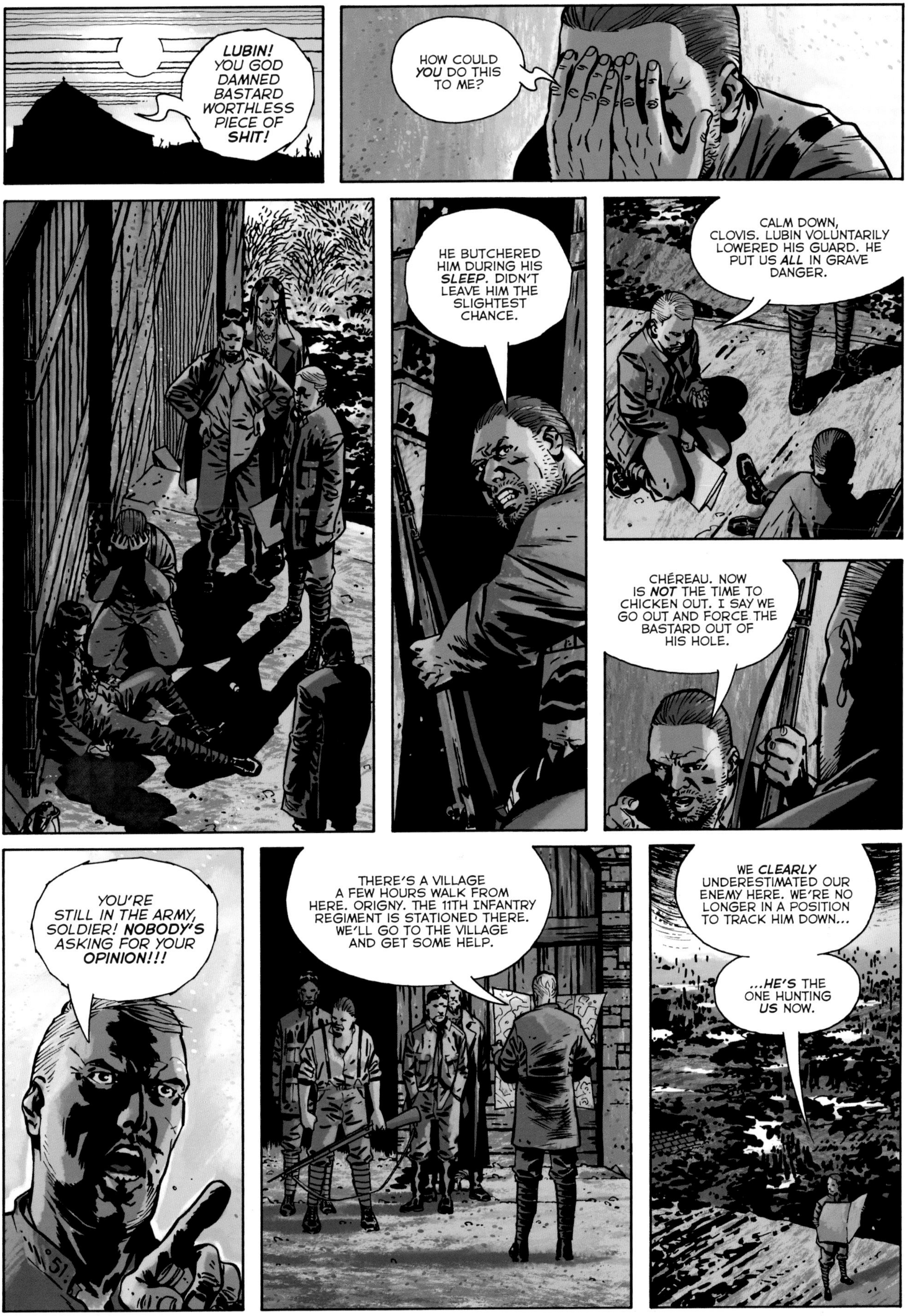
LUBIN! YOU GOD DAMNED BASTARD WORTHLESS PIECE OF SHIT!
HOW COULD YOU DO THIS TO ME?
HE BUTCHERED HIM DURING HIS SLEEP. DIDN'T LEAVE HIM THE SLIGHTEST CHANCE.
CALM DOWN, CLOVIS. LUBIN VOLUNTARILY LOWERED HIS GUARD. HE PUT US ALL IN GRAVE DANGER.
CHÉREAU. NOW IS NOT THE TIME TO CHICKEN OUT. I SAY WE GO OUT AND FORCE THE BASTARD OUT OF HIS HOLE.
YOU'RE STILL IN THE ARMY, SOLDIER! NOBODY'S ASKING FOR YOUR OPINION!!!
THERE'S A VILLAGE A FEW HOURS WALK FROM HERE. ORIGNY. THE 11TH INFANTRY REGIMENT IS STATIONED THERE. WE'LL GO TO THE VILLAGE AND GET SOME HELP.
WE CLEARLY UNDERESTIMATED OUR ENEMY HERE. WE'RE NO LONGER IN A POSITION TO TRACK HIM DOWN...
...HE'S THE ONE HUNTING US NOW.

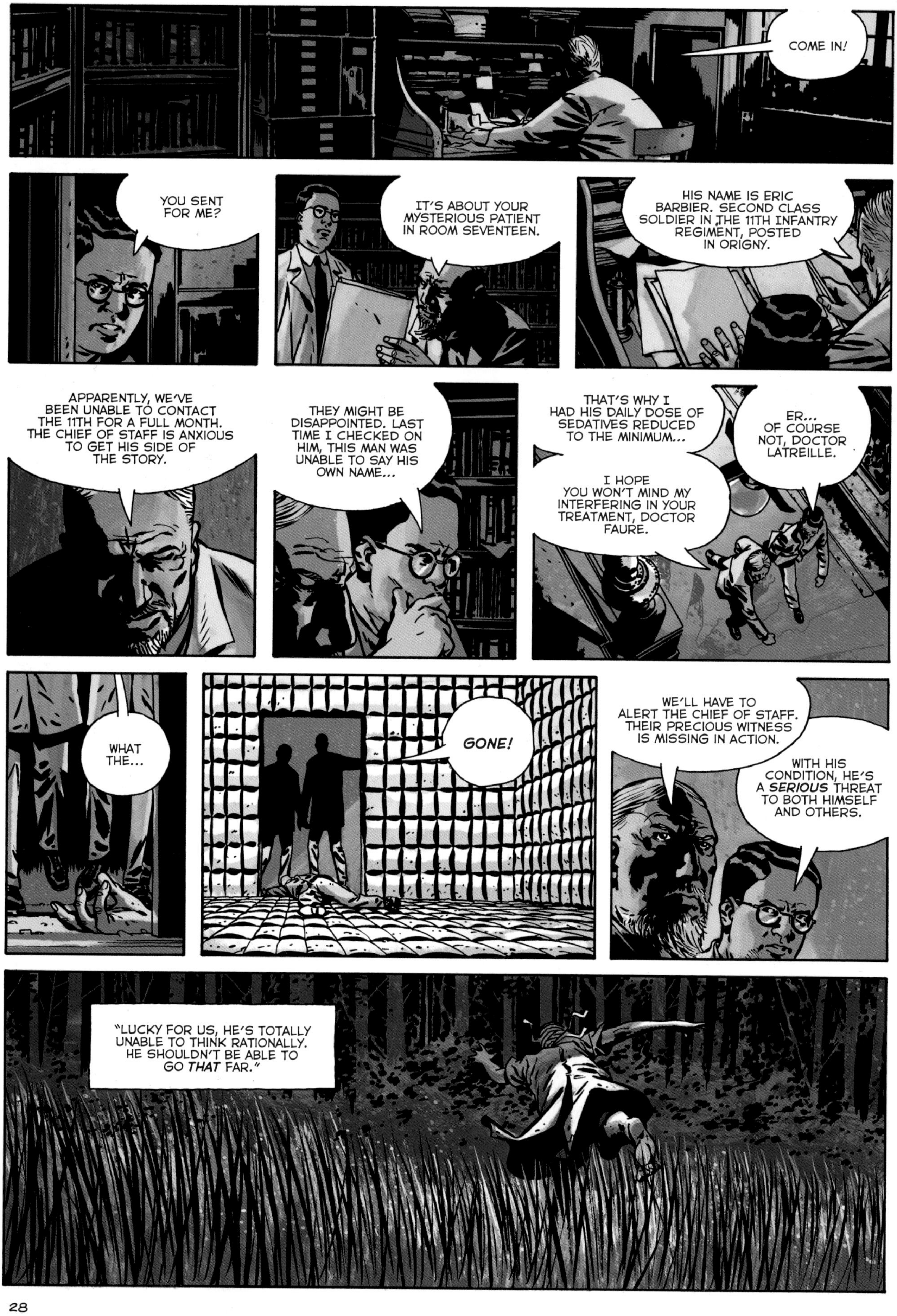
COME IN!
YOU SENT FOR ME?
IT'S ABOUT YOUR MYSTERIOUS PATIENT IN ROOM SEVENTEEN.
HIS NAME IS ERIC BARBIER. SECOND CLASS SOLDIER IN THE 11TH INFANTRY REGIMENT, POSTED IN ORIGNY.
APPARENTLY, WE'VE BEEN UNABLE TO CONTACT THE 11TH FOR A FULL MONTH. THE CHIEF OF STAFF IS ANXIOUS TO GET HIS SIDE OF THE STORY.
THEY MIGHT BE DISAPPOINTED. LAST TIME I CHECKED ON HIM, THIS MAN WAS UNABLE TO SAY HIS OWN NAME...
THAT'S WHY I HAD HIS DAILY DOSE OF SEDATIVES REDUCED TO THE MINIMUM...
I HOPE YOU WON'T MIND MY INTERFERING IN YOUR TREATMENT, DOCTOR FAURE.
ER... OF COURSE NOT, DOCTOR LATREILLE.
WHAT THE...
GONE!
WE'LL HAVE TO ALERT THE CHIEF OF STAFF. THEIR PRECIOUS WITNESS IS MISSING IN ACTION.
WITH HIS CONDITION, HE'S A SERIOUS THREAT TO BOTH HIMSELF AND OTHERS.
"LUCKY FOR US, HE'S TOTALLY UNABLE TO THINK RATIONALLY. HE SHOULDN'T BE ABLE TO GO THAT FAR."

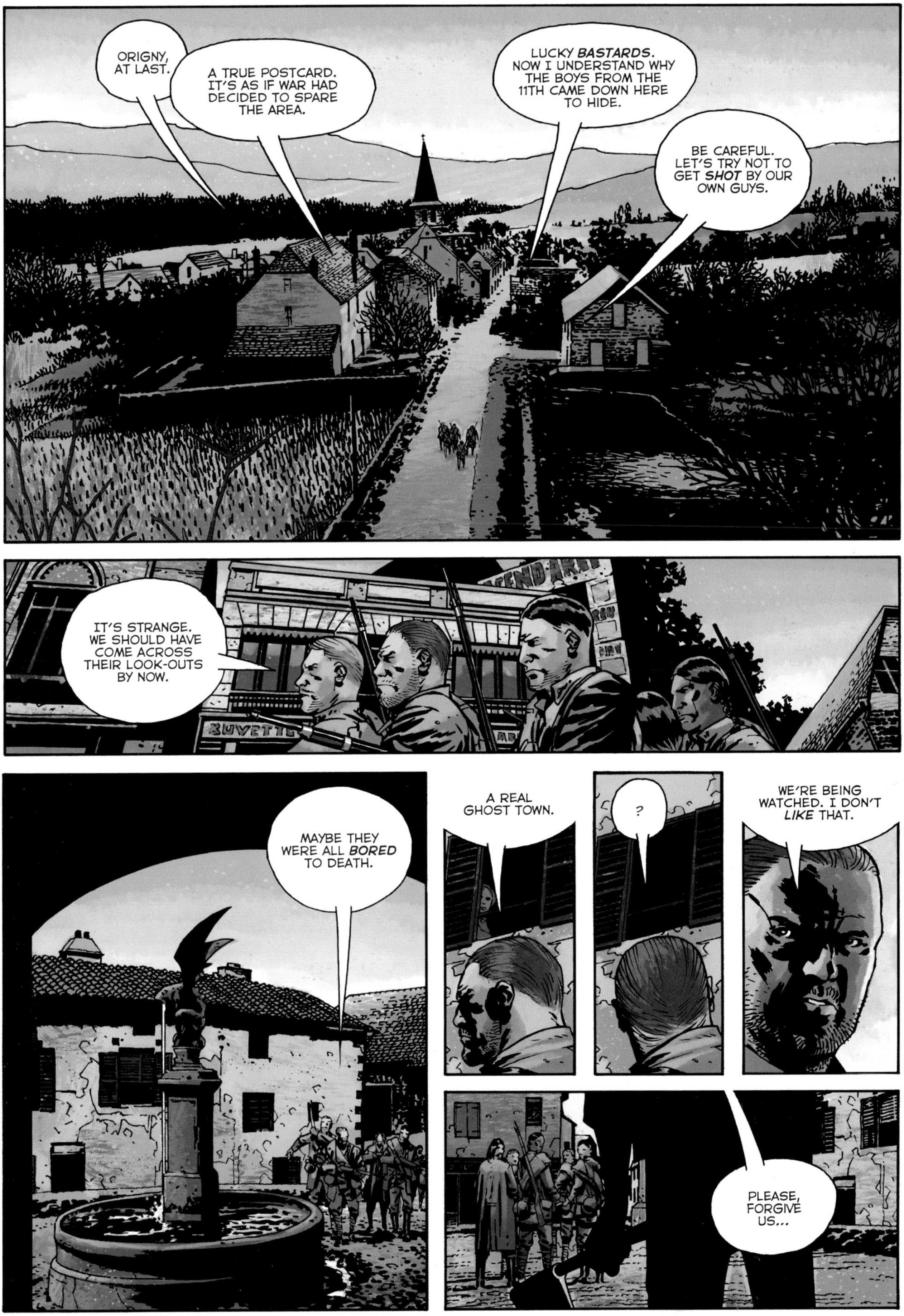
ORIGNY, AT LAST.
A TRUE POSTCARD. IT'S AS IF WAR HAD DECIDED TO SPARE THE AREA.
LUCKY **BASTARDS.** NOW I UNDERSTAND WHY THE BOYS FROM THE 11TH CAME DOWN HERE TO HIDE.
BE CAREFUL. LET'S TRY NOT TO GET **SHOT** BY OUR OWN GUYS.
IT'S STRANGE. WE SHOULD HAVE COME ACROSS THEIR LOOK-OUTS BY NOW.
MAYBE THEY WERE ALL ***BORED*** TO DEATH.
A REAL GHOST TOWN.
?
WE'RE BEING WATCHED. I DON'T ***LIKE*** THAT.
PLEASE, FORGIVE US...

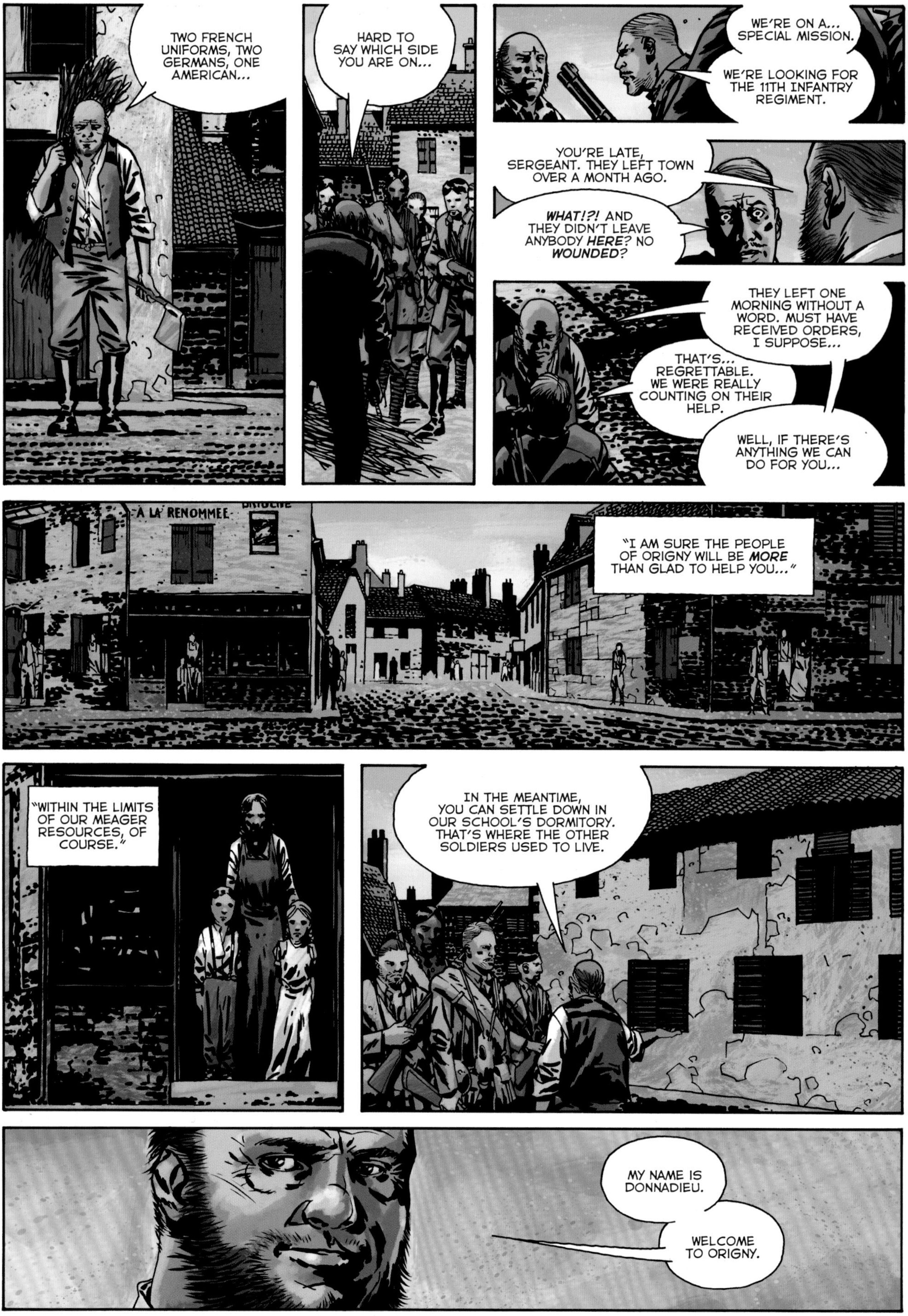
TWO FRENCH UNIFORMS, TWO GERMANS, ONE AMERICAN...
HARD TO SAY WHICH SIDE YOU ARE ON...
WE'RE ON A... SPECIAL MISSION.
WE'RE LOOKING FOR THE 11TH INFANTRY REGIMENT.
YOU'RE LATE, SERGEANT. THEY LEFT TOWN OVER A MONTH AGO.
WHAT!?! AND THEY DIDN'T LEAVE ANYBODY HERE? NO WOUNDED?
THEY LEFT ONE MORNING WITHOUT A WORD. MUST HAVE RECEIVED ORDERS, I SUPPOSE...
THAT'S... REGRETTABLE. WE WERE REALLY COUNTING ON THEIR HELP.
WELL, IF THERE'S ANYTHING WE CAN DO FOR YOU...
A LA RENOMMEE
"I AM SURE THE PEOPLE OF ORIGNY WILL BE MORE THAN GLAD TO HELP YOU..."
"WITHIN THE LIMITS OF OUR MEAGER RESOURCES, OF COURSE."
IN THE MEANTIME, YOU CAN SETTLE DOWN IN OUR SCHOOL'S DORMITORY. THAT'S WHERE THE OTHER SOLDIERS USED TO LIVE.
MY NAME IS DONNADIEU.
WELCOME TO ORIGNY.

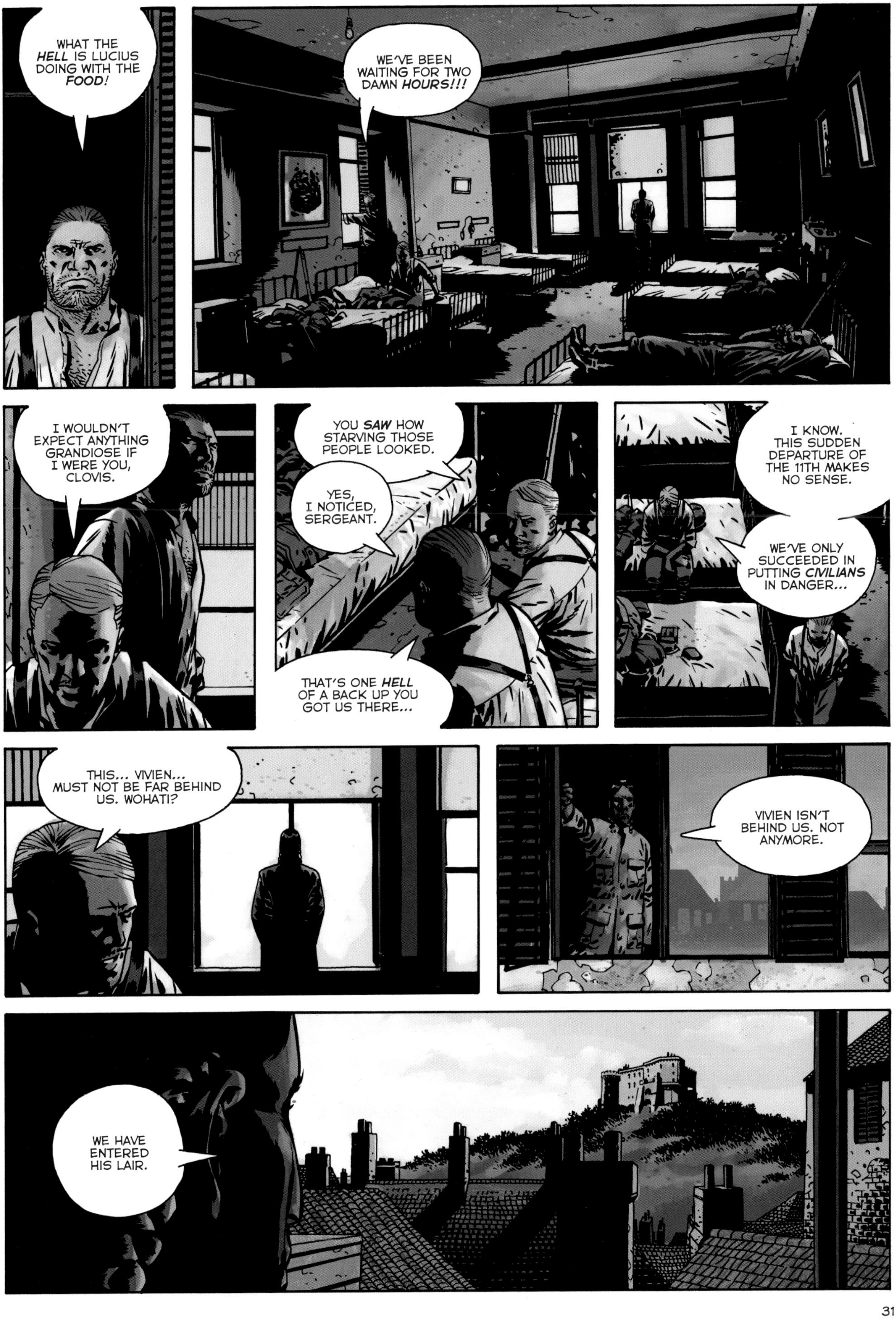
WHAT THE HELL IS LUCIUS DOING WITH THE FOOD!
WE'VE BEEN WAITING FOR TWO DAMN HOURS!!!
I WOULDN'T EXPECT ANYTHING GRANDIOSE IF I WERE YOU, CLOVIS.
YOU SAW HOW STARVING THOSE PEOPLE LOOKED.
YES, I NOTICED, SERGEANT.
THAT'S ONE HELL OF A BACK UP YOU GOT US THERE...
I KNOW. THIS SUDDEN DEPARTURE OF THE 11TH MAKES NO SENSE.
WE'VE ONLY SUCCEEDED IN PUTTING CIVILIANS IN DANGER...
THIS... VIVIEN... MUST NOT BE FAR BEHIND US. WOHATI?
VIVIEN ISN'T BEHIND US. NOT ANYMORE.
WE HAVE ENTERED HIS LAIR.

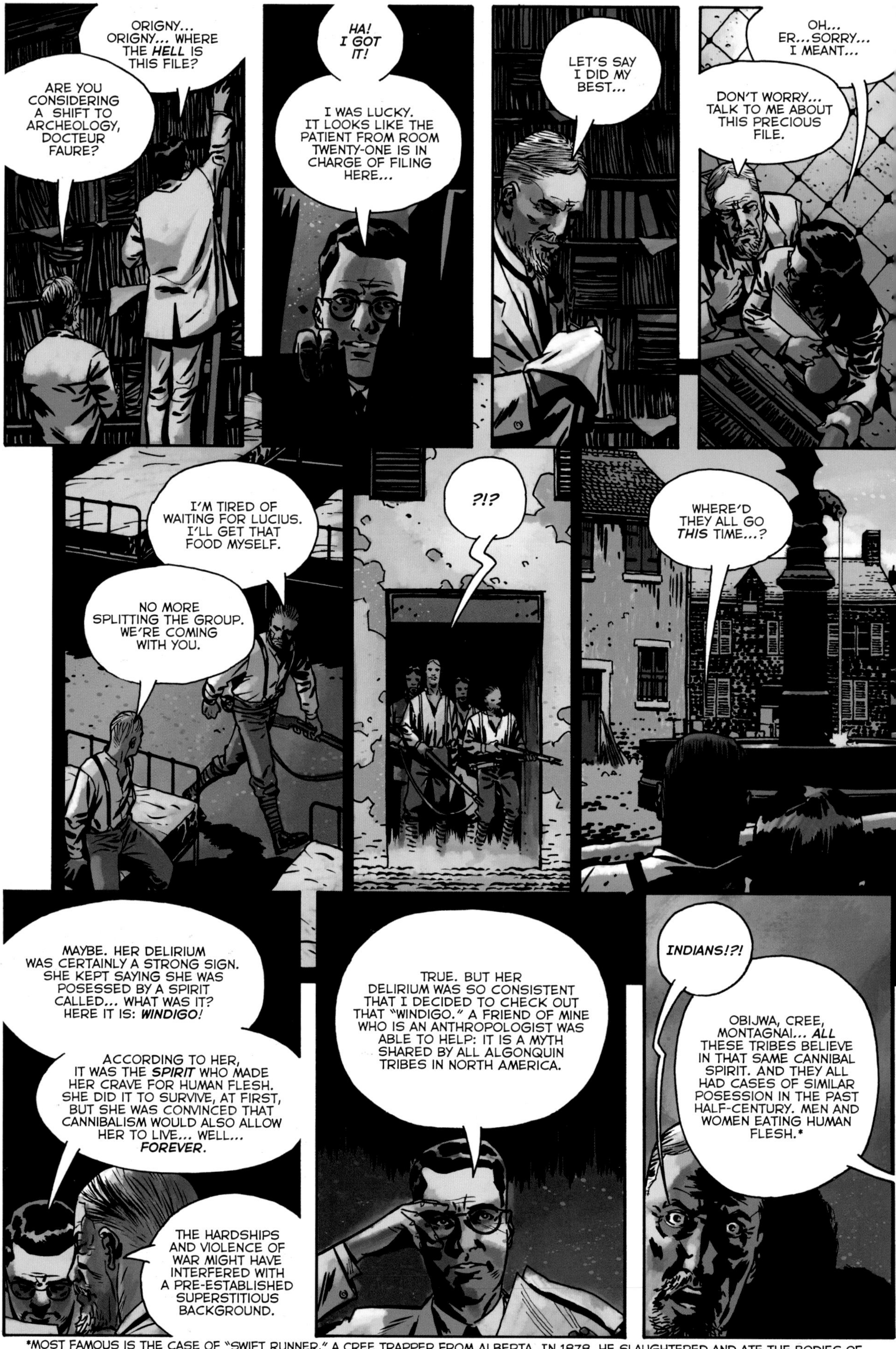
ORIGNY... ORIGNY... WHERE THE HELL IS THIS FILE?
ARE YOU CONSIDERING A SHIFT TO ARCHEOLOGY, DOCTEUR FAURE?
HA! I GOT IT!
I WAS LUCKY. IT LOOKS LIKE THE PATIENT FROM ROOM TWENTY-ONE IS IN CHARGE OF FILING HERE...
LET'S SAY I DID MY BEST...
OH... ER...SORRY... I MEANT...
DON'T WORRY... TALK TO ME ABOUT THIS PRECIOUS FILE.
I'M TIRED OF WAITING FOR LUCIUS. I'LL GET THAT FOOD MYSELF.
NO MORE SPLITTING THE GROUP. WE'RE COMING WITH YOU.
?!?
WHERE'D THEY ALL GO THIS TIME...?
MAYBE. HER DELIRIUM WAS CERTAINLY A STRONG SIGN. SHE KEPT SAYING SHE WAS POSESSED BY A SPIRIT CALLED... WHAT WAS IT? HERE IT IS: WINDIGO!
ACCORDING TO HER, IT WAS THE SPIRIT WHO MADE HER CRAVE FOR HUMAN FLESH. SHE DID IT TO SURVIVE, AT FIRST, BUT SHE WAS CONVINCED THAT CANNIBALISM WOULD ALSO ALLOW HER TO LIVE... WELL... FOREVER.
THE HARDSHIPS AND VIOLENCE OF WAR MIGHT HAVE INTERFERED WITH A PRE-ESTABLISHED SUPERSTITIOUS BACKGROUND.
TRUE. BUT HER DELIRIUM WAS SO CONSISTENT THAT I DECIDED TO CHECK OUT THAT "WINDIGO." A FRIEND OF MINE WHO IS AN ANTHROPOLOGIST WAS ABLE TO HELP: IT IS A MYTH SHARED BY ALL ALGONQUIN TRIBES IN NORTH AMERICA.
INDIANS!?!
OBIJWA, CREE, MONTAGNAI... ALL THESE TRIBES BELIEVE IN THAT SAME CANNIBAL SPIRIT. AND THEY ALL HAD CASES OF SIMILAR POSESSION IN THE PAST HALF-CENTURY. MEN AND WOMEN EATING HUMAN FLESH.*

*MOST FAMOUS IS THE CASE OF "SWIFT RUNNER," A CREE TRAPPER FROM ALBERTA. IN 1878, HE SLAUGHTERED AND ATE THE BODIES OF HIS WIFE AND FIVE OF HIS CHILDREN BEFORE BEING ARRESTED AND SENTENCED TO DEATH. THIS IS GENERALLY THOUGHT TO BE THE FIRST DOCUMENTED CASE OF "WINDIGO PSYCHOSIS."

IT'S THE NAME OF THAT VILLAGE THAT RANG A BELL. *ORIGNY.*

TWO YEARS AGO, A YOUNG WOMAN FROM THAT SAME VILLAGE WAS BROUGHT HERE. GERVAISE LEROUX. A STRANGE CASE, REALLY.

WITH NO APPARENT MOTIVE, SHE MURDERED A YOUNG SOLDIER. AFTER THAT, SHE PROCEEDED TO... *COOK* THE BODY. BY THE TIME SHE WAS FOUND AND ARRESTED, SHE HAD ALREADY... CONSUMED MUCH OF HIS FLESH.

IT WAS LATER DISCOVERED THAT SHE WAS ALSO RESPONSIBLE FOR THE PAST DISAPPEARANCES OF *SEVERAL* OTHER SOLDIERS.

A CASE OF *CANNIBALISM?* I AM NOT THAT SURPRISED... BECAUSE OF THE WAR, MANY VILLAGES WERE COMPLETELY CUT OFF FOR MONTHS. WITH NO FOOD SUPPLIES AT ALL...

GERVAISE LEROUX DID SHOW SIGNS OF PAST MALNUTRITION.... HOWEVER, AT THE TIME OF HER CRIMES, SHE HAD ALREADY LEFT ORIGNY. SHE WAS A COOK IN THE ARMY, AND THEREFORE HAD ACCESS TO *PLENTY* OF FOOD SUPPLIES.

WHAT THEN? DEMENTIA PRAECOX? A *SCHIZOPHRENIC*, AS THEY'RE CALLED NOW?

WOHATI, DO YOU...

WOHATI???

HE WAS HERE TEN SECONDS AGO! *WHAT THE HELL IS GOING ON?!?*

THIS IS GETTING BETTER BY THE MINUTE.

YOU HEAR THAT NOISE?

COME ON, DOCTOR FAURE, DON'T TELL ME THAT YOU ACTUALLY *BELIEVE* IN THIS MYTH...

NO, OF COURSE. BUT IT SEEMS INTERESTING TO ME THAT SEVERAL INDIVIDUALS EXPOSED TO THE SAME FOLKLORE DEVELOPED SIMILAR SPECIFIC SYMPTOMS.

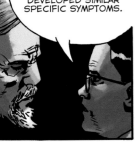

A CULTURAL BELIEF GENERATING A PATHOLOGY SPECIFIC TO A GIVEN COMMUNITY... INTERESTING...

THERE'S ONLY ONE PROBLEM...

I'M AFRAID THE CLOSEST ALGONQUIAN TRIBE LIVES MORE THAN 10,000 MILES AWAY FROM ORIGNY.

TRUE. I WONDER HOW THAT STORY ENDED UP ON THE OTHER SIDE OF THE WORLD, IN THE TWISTED MIND OF A GIRL FRESH OUT OF HER HOMETOWN.

STILL, YOU HAVE TO ADMIT THE WHOLE THING IS STRANGE... THOSE CONSISTENT DELIRIUM SCENARIOS... AND THOSE BITE MARKS ON BARBIER'S BODY, WHO WAS ALSO STATIONED IN ORIGNY.

THAT'S ONE MORE MYSTERY, INDEED. BUT WHAT HAPPENED TO THAT PATIENT OF YOURS?

SHE... SHE DIDN'T REACT WELL TO HER CONFINEMENT. SHE MANAGED TO HANG HERSELF IN HER CELL AFTER JUST TWO WEEKS.

WELL, POSSESSION OR MENTAL DISORDER, IT LOOKS LIKE WE'RE GONNA HAVE TO WAIT FOR THE END OF THE WAR BEFORE WE KNOW WHAT THIS IS ALL *REALLY* ABOUT.*

*IT IS GENERALLY ACCEPTED TODAY THAT THE "WINDIGO PSYCHOSIS" BELONGS TO THE GROUP OF CULTURE-BOUND SYNDROMES, AS DESCRIBED IN THE AMERICAN CLASSIFICATION OF MENTAL DISORDERS DSM-IV.

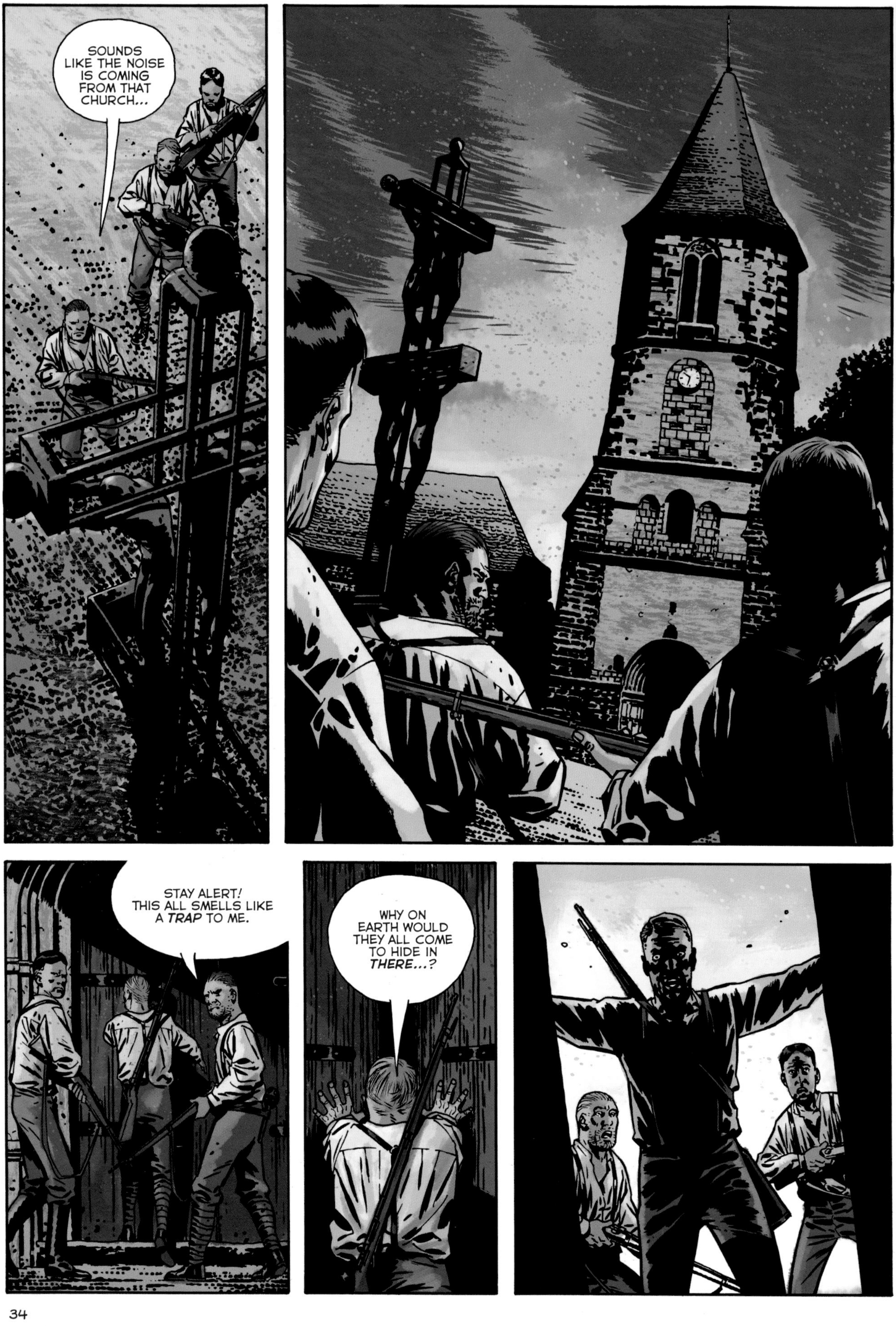
SOUNDS LIKE THE NOISE IS COMING FROM THAT CHURCH...
STAY ALERT! THIS ALL SMELLS LIKE A *TRAP* TO ME.
WHY ON EARTH WOULD THEY ALL COME TO HIDE IN *THERE...?*

HOLY MOTHER OF GOD...

AH, YOU'RE HERE...

RIGHT ON TIME FOR DINNER...

YOU SICK *FUCK*... DON'T COME ANY CLOSER OR I'LL SHOOT.

SERGEANT! THEY'RE COMING FROM EVERYWHERE!!

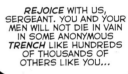

REJOICE WITH US, SERGEANT. YOU AND YOUR MEN WILL NOT DIE IN VAIN IN SOME ANONYMOUS *TRENCH* LIKE HUNDREDS OF THOUSANDS OF OTHERS LIKE YOU...

"INSTEAD YOU ALLOW OUR LITTLE COMMUNITY TO SURVIVE... AND *YOU* WILL SURVIVE THROUGH US TOO."

WOHATI WAS TELLING THE TRUTH. ONLY HE FORGOT TO MENTION HIS *MONSTER* HAD BEEN BUSY *REPRODUCING*.

SERGEANT, WE HAVEN'T GOT MANY OPTIONS. WE NEED TO FORCE OUR WAY THROUGH.

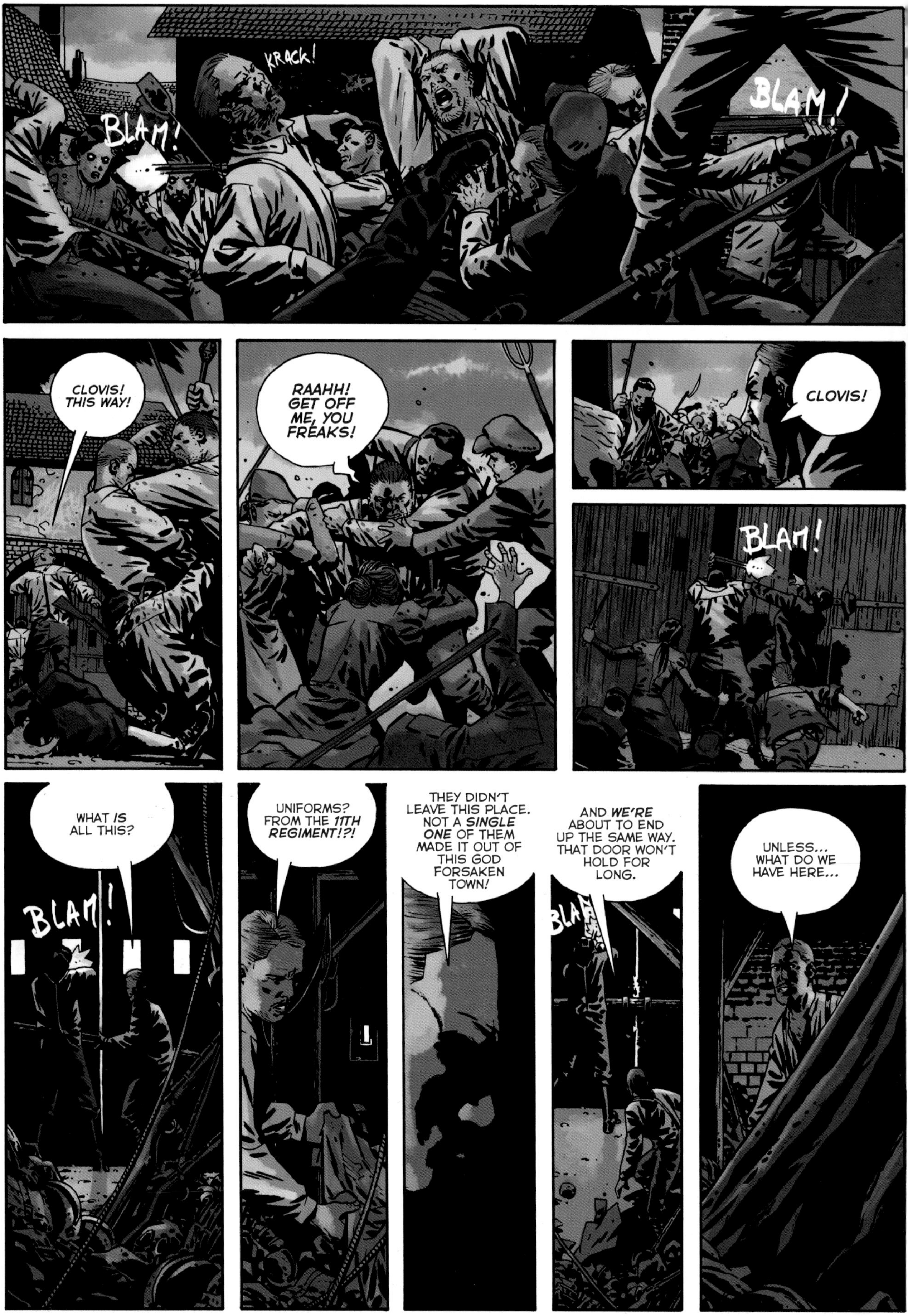
KRACK!
BLAM!
BLAM!
CLOVIS! THIS WAY!
RAAHH! GET OFF ME, YOU FREAKS!
CLOVIS!
BLAM!
WHAT IS ALL THIS?
BLAM!
UNIFORMS? FROM THE 11TH REGIMENT!?!
THEY DIDN'T LEAVE THIS PLACE. NOT A SINGLE ONE OF THEM MADE IT OUT OF THIS GOD FORSAKEN TOWN!
AND WE'RE ABOUT TO END UP THE SAME WAY. THAT DOOR WON'T HOLD FOR LONG.
UNLESS... WHAT DO WE HAVE HERE...

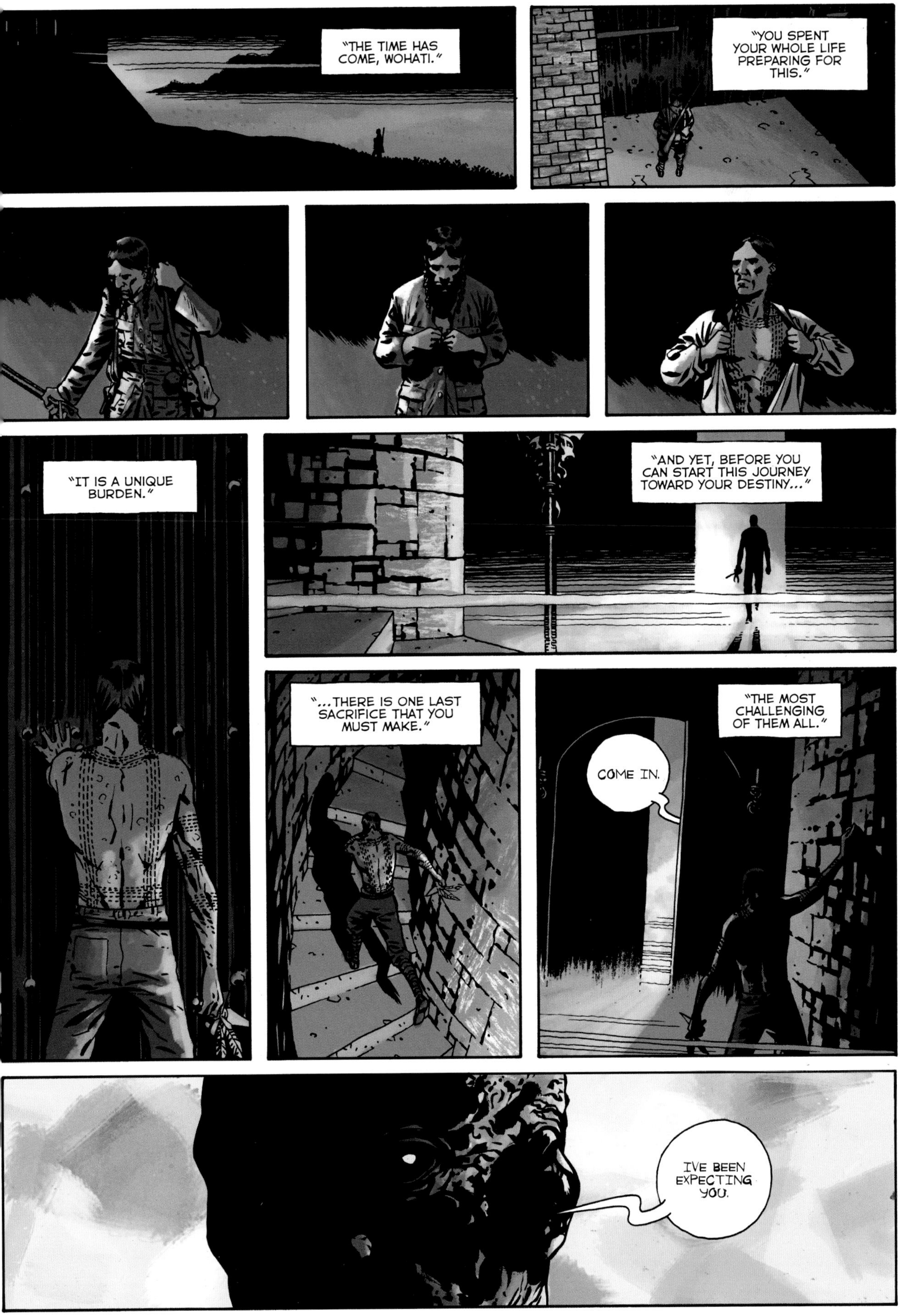
"THE TIME HAS COME, WOHATI."
"YOU SPENT YOUR WHOLE LIFE PREPARING FOR THIS."
"IT IS A UNIQUE BURDEN."
"AND YET, BEFORE YOU CAN START THIS JOURNEY TOWARD YOUR DESTINY..."
"...THERE IS ONE LAST SACRIFICE THAT YOU MUST MAKE."
"THE MOST CHALLENGING OF THEM ALL."
COME IN.
I'VE BEEN EXPECTING YOU.

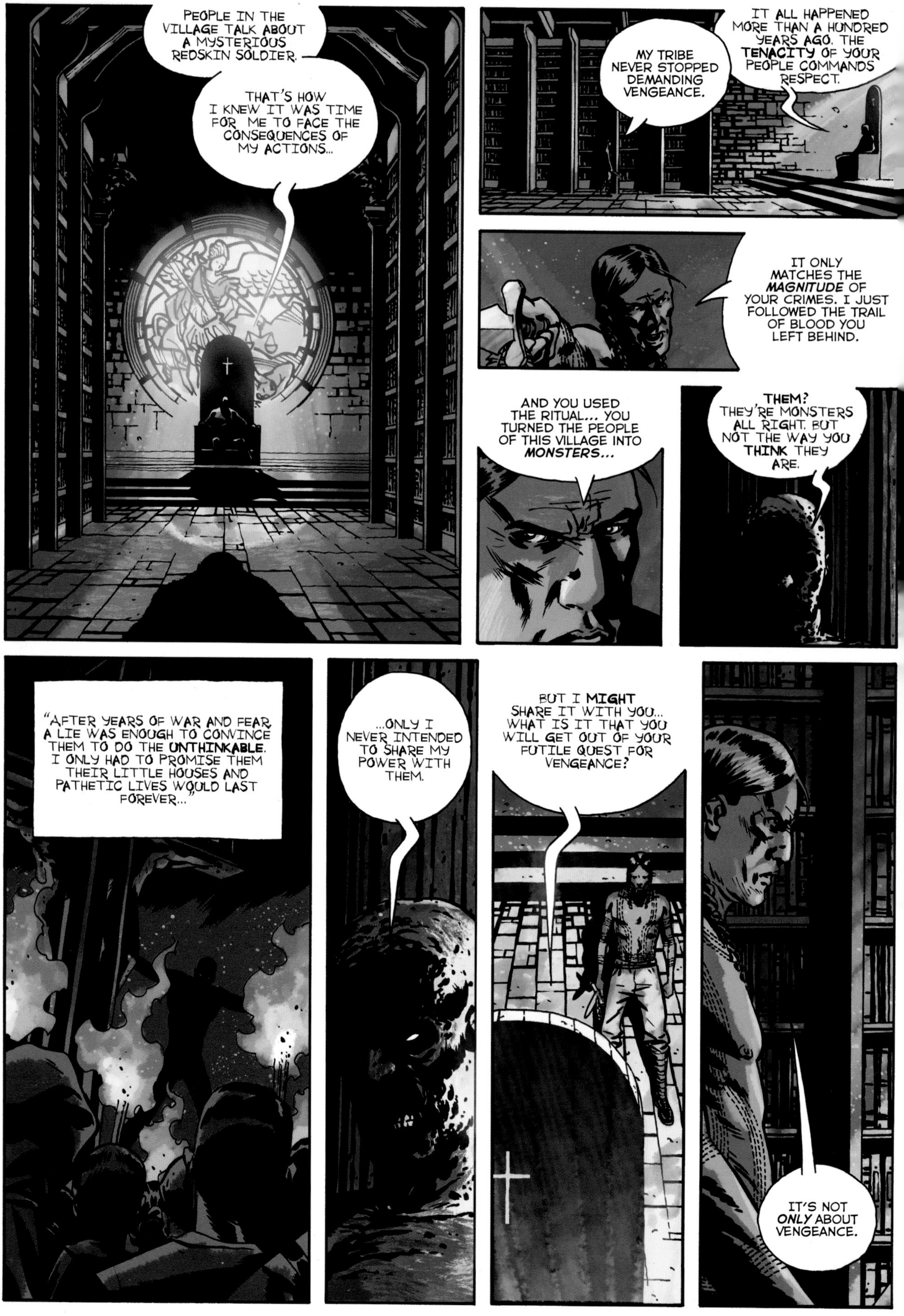
PEOPLE IN THE VILLAGE TALK ABOUT A MYSTERIOUS REDSKIN SOLDIER.
THAT'S HOW I KNEW IT WAS TIME FOR ME TO FACE THE CONSEQUENCES OF MY ACTIONS...
MY TRIBE NEVER STOPPED DEMANDING VENGEANCE.
IT ALL HAPPENED MORE THAN A HUNDRED YEARS AGO. THE TENACITY OF YOUR PEOPLE COMMANDS RESPECT.
IT ONLY MATCHES THE MAGNITUDE OF YOUR CRIMES. I JUST FOLLOWED THE TRAIL OF BLOOD YOU LEFT BEHIND.
AND YOU USED THE RITUAL... YOU TURNED THE PEOPLE OF THIS VILLAGE INTO MONSTERS...
THEM? THEY'RE MONSTERS ALL RIGHT. BUT NOT THE WAY YOU THINK THEY ARE.
"AFTER YEARS OF WAR AND FEAR, A LIE WAS ENOUGH TO CONVINCE THEM TO DO THE UNTHINKABLE. I ONLY HAD TO PROMISE THEM THEIR LITTLE HOUSES AND PATHETIC LIVES WOULD LAST FOREVER..."
...ONLY I NEVER INTENDED TO SHARE MY POWER WITH THEM.
BUT I MIGHT SHARE IT WITH YOU... WHAT IS IT THAT YOU WILL GET OUT OF YOUR FUTILE QUEST FOR VENGEANCE?
IT'S NOT ONLY ABOUT VENGEANCE.

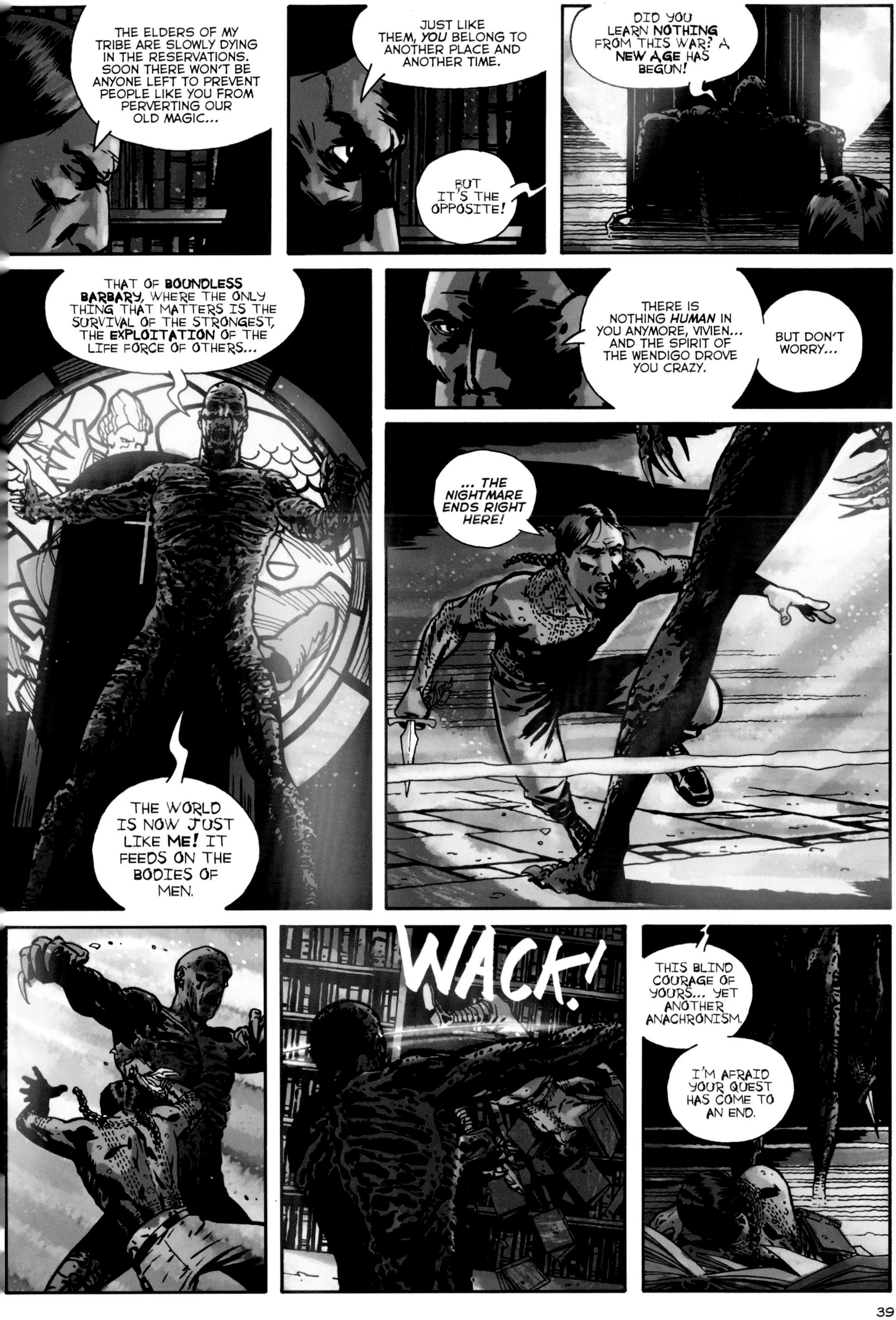
THE ELDERS OF MY TRIBE ARE SLOWLY DYING IN THE RESERVATIONS. SOON THERE WON'T BE ANYONE LEFT TO PREVENT PEOPLE LIKE YOU FROM PERVERTING OUR OLD MAGIC...
JUST LIKE THEM, YOU BELONG TO ANOTHER PLACE AND ANOTHER TIME.
BUT IT'S THE OPPOSITE!
DID YOU LEARN NOTHING FROM THIS WAR? A NEW AGE HAS BEGUN!
THAT OF BOUNDLESS BARBARY, WHERE THE ONLY THING THAT MATTERS IS THE SURVIVAL OF THE STRONGEST, THE EXPLOITATION OF THE LIFE FORCE OF OTHERS...
THE WORLD IS NOW JUST LIKE ME! IT FEEDS ON THE BODIES OF MEN.
THERE IS NOTHING HUMAN IN YOU ANYMORE, VIVIEN... AND THE SPIRIT OF THE WENDIGO DROVE YOU CRAZY.
BUT DON'T WORRY...
... THE NIGHTMARE ENDS RIGHT HERE!
WACK!
THIS BLIND COURAGE OF YOURS... YET ANOTHER ANACHRONISM.
I'M AFRAID YOUR QUEST HAS COME TO AN END.

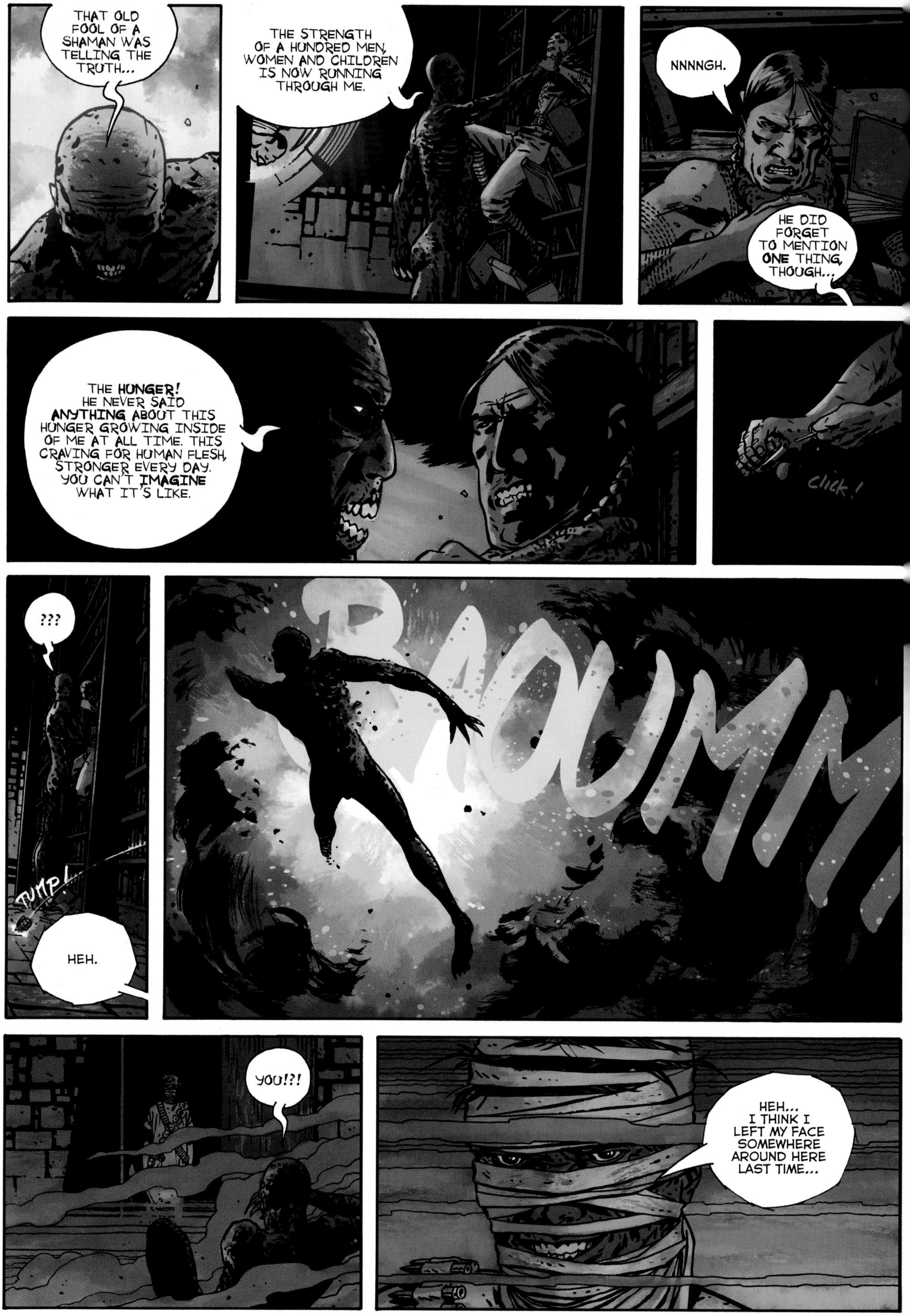
THAT OLD FOOL OF A SHAMAN WAS TELLING THE TRUTH...
THE STRENGTH OF A HUNDRED MEN, WOMEN AND CHILDREN IS NOW RUNNING THROUGH ME.
NNNNGH.
HE DID FORGET TO MENTION ONE THING, THOUGH...
THE HUNGER! HE NEVER SAID ANYTHING ABOUT THIS HUNGER GROWING INSIDE OF ME AT ALL TIME. THIS CRAVING FOR HUMAN FLESH, STRONGER EVERY DAY. YOU CAN'T IMAGINE WHAT IT'S LIKE.
CLICK!
???
TUMP!
HEH.
BAOUMM
YOU!?!
HEH... I THINK I LEFT MY FACE SOMEWHERE AROUND HERE LAST TIME...

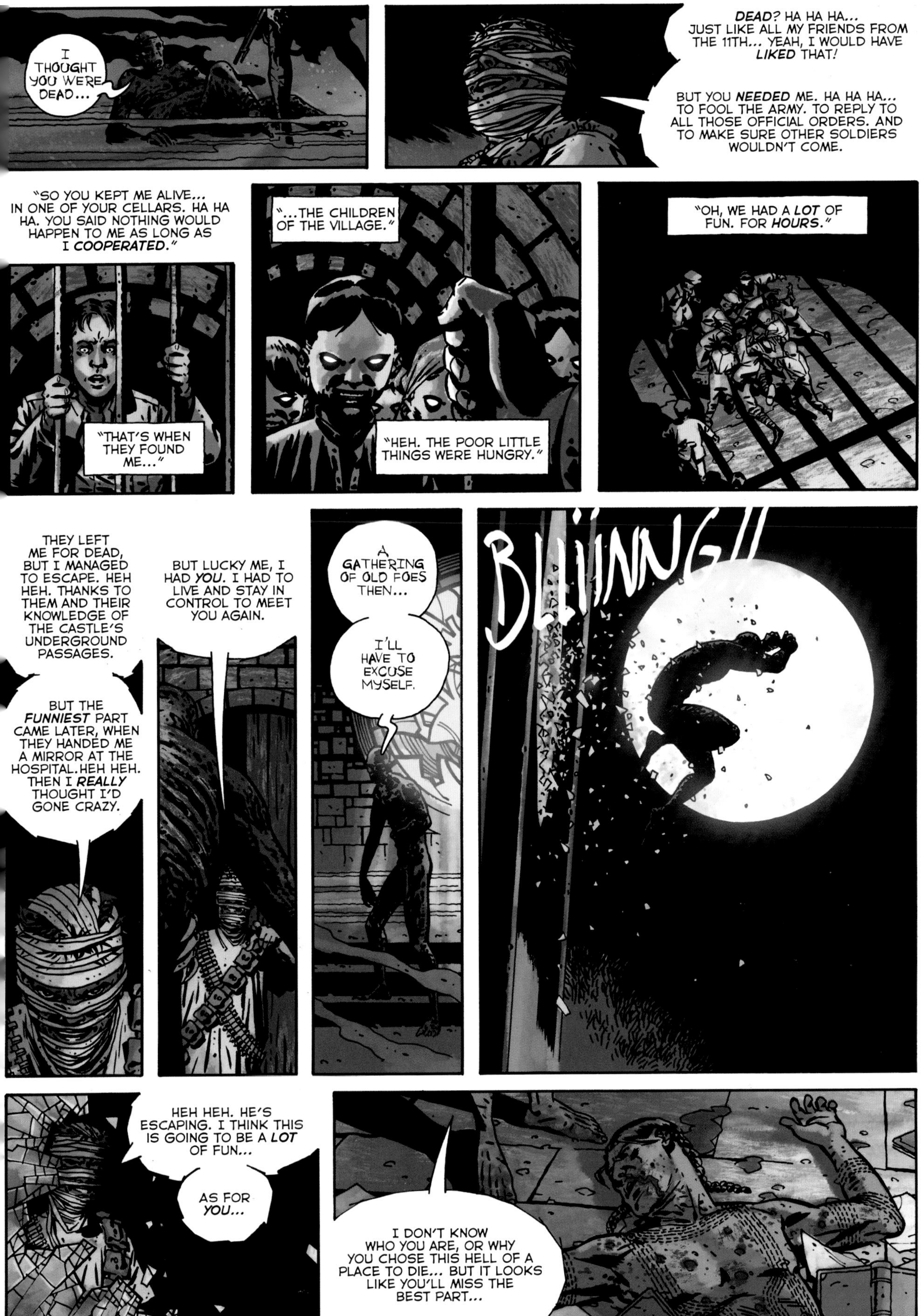
I THOUGHT YOU WERE DEAD...
DEAD? HA HA HA... JUST LIKE ALL MY FRIENDS FROM THE 11TH... YEAH, I WOULD HAVE LIKED THAT!
BUT YOU NEEDED ME. HA HA HA... TO FOOL THE ARMY. TO REPLY TO ALL THOSE OFFICIAL ORDERS. AND TO MAKE SURE OTHER SOLDIERS WOULDN'T COME.
"SO YOU KEPT ME ALIVE... IN ONE OF YOUR CELLARS. HA HA HA. YOU SAID NOTHING WOULD HAPPEN TO ME AS LONG AS I COOPERATED."
"THAT'S WHEN THEY FOUND ME..."
"...THE CHILDREN OF THE VILLAGE."
"HEH. THE POOR LITTLE THINGS WERE HUNGRY."
"OH, WE HAD A LOT OF FUN. FOR HOURS."
THEY LEFT ME FOR DEAD, BUT I MANAGED TO ESCAPE. HEH HEH. THANKS TO THEM AND THEIR KNOWLEDGE OF THE CASTLE'S UNDERGROUND PASSAGES.
BUT THE FUNNIEST PART CAME LATER, WHEN THEY HANDED ME A MIRROR AT THE HOSPITAL. HEH HEH. THEN I REALLY THOUGHT I'D GONE CRAZY.
BUT LUCKY ME, I HAD YOU. I HAD TO LIVE AND STAY IN CONTROL TO MEET YOU AGAIN.
A GATHERING OF OLD FOES THEN...
I'LL HAVE TO EXCUSE MYSELF.
BLIINNG!!
HEH HEH. HE'S ESCAPING. I THINK THIS IS GOING TO BE A LOT OF FUN...
AS FOR YOU...
I DON'T KNOW WHO YOU ARE, OR WHY YOU CHOSE THIS HELL OF A PLACE TO DIE... BUT IT LOOKS LIKE YOU'LL MISS THE BEST PART...

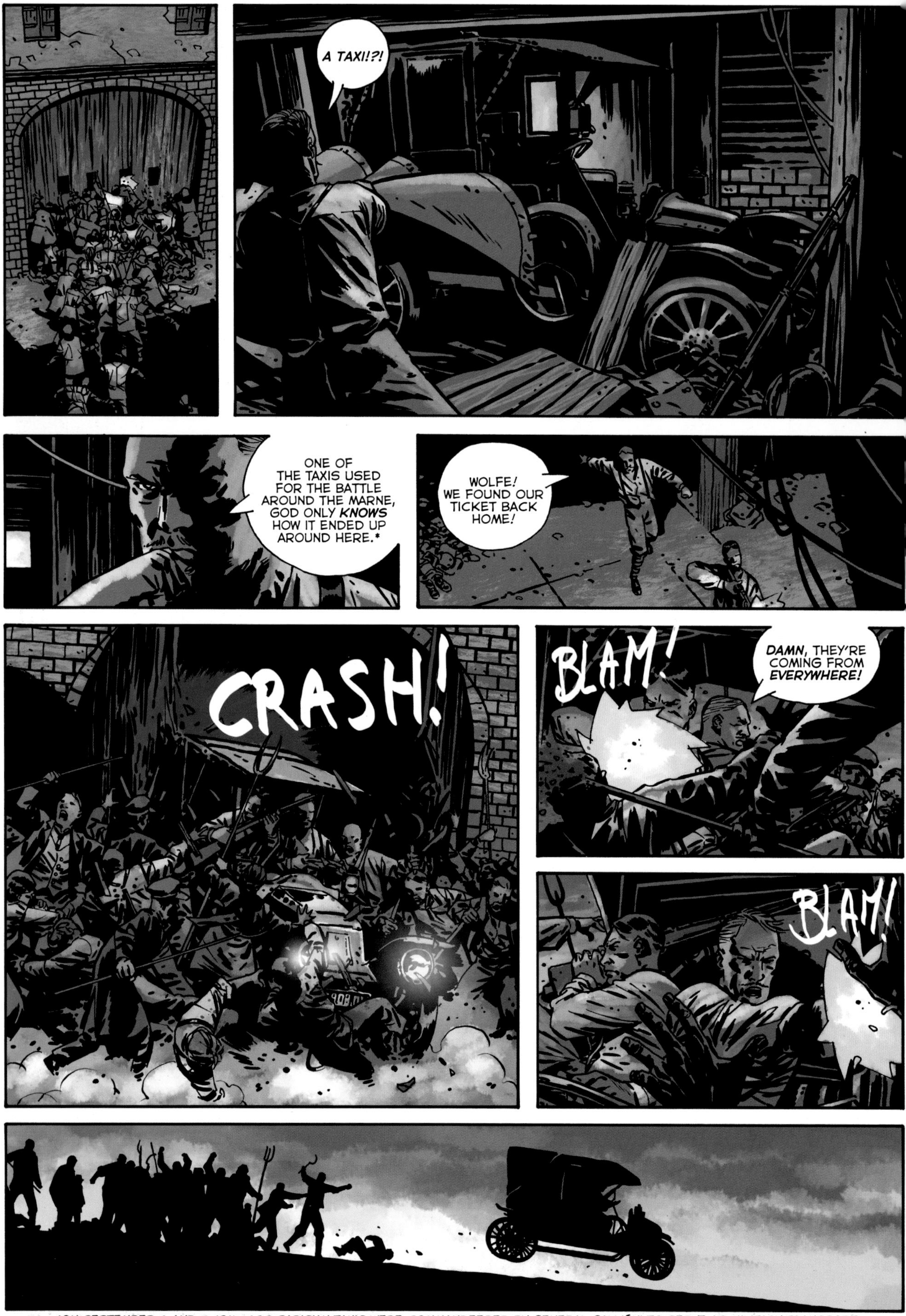
A TAXI!?!
ONE OF THE TAXIS USED FOR THE BATTLE AROUND THE MARNE, GOD ONLY KNOWS HOW IT ENDED UP AROUND HERE.*
WOLFE! WE FOUND OUR TICKET BACK HOME!
CRASH!
BLAM!
DAMN, THEY'RE COMING FROM EVERYWHERE!
BLAM!

*ON SEPTEMBER 6 AND 7, 1914, 600 PARISIAN TAXIS WERE COMMANDEERED BY GENERAL GALLIÉNI TO SERVE AS MILITARY TRANSPORT FOR THE MEN OF THE 7TH INFANTRY DIVISION. THIS OPERATION ALLOWED 6000 SOLDIERS TO MOVE TO THE FRONTLINES, CHANGING THE COURSE OF THE FIRST BATTLE OF THE MARNE IN FAVOR OF THE FRENCH ARMY.

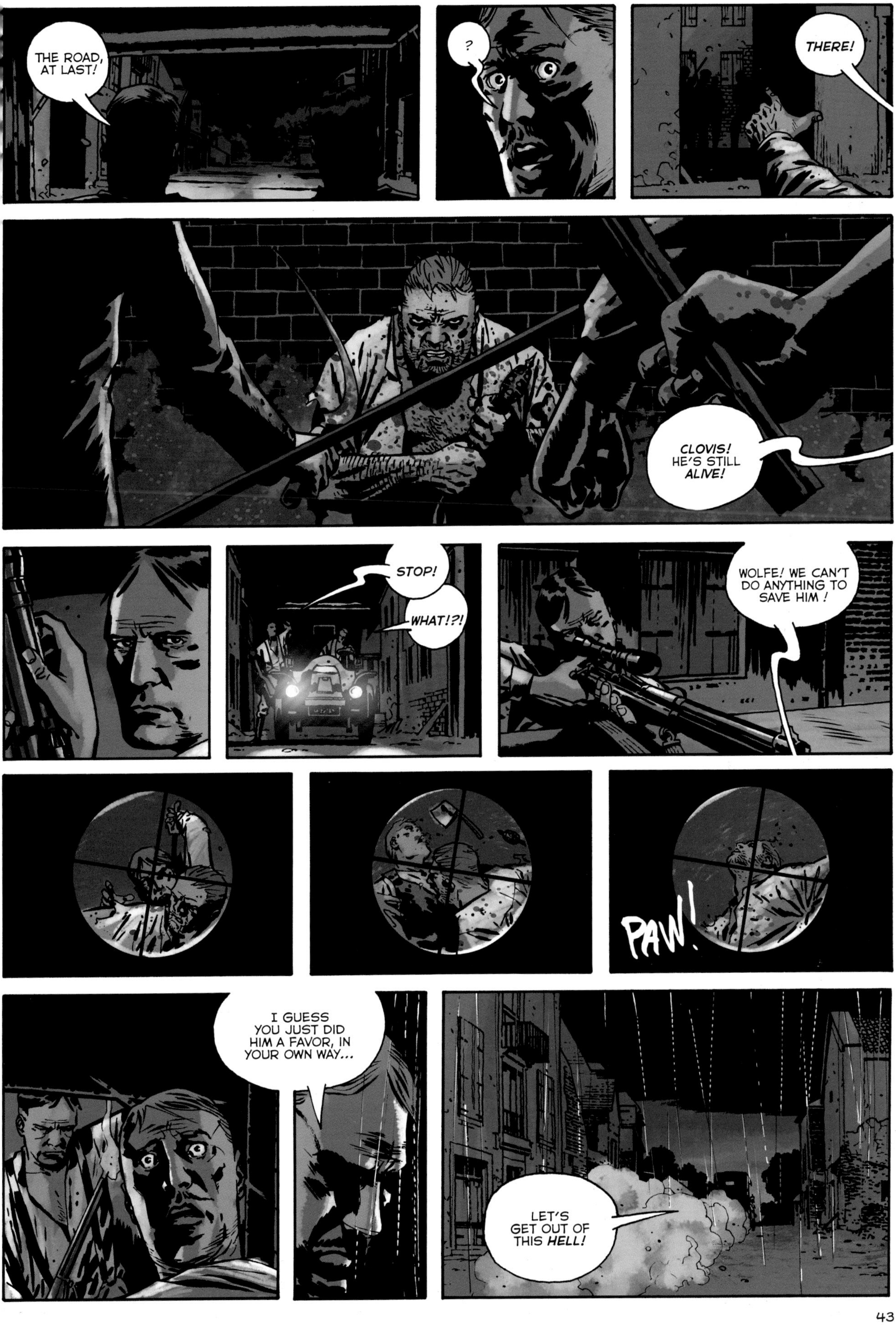
THE ROAD, AT LAST!
?
THERE!
CLOVIS! HE'S STILL ALIVE!
STOP!
WHAT!?!
WOLFE! WE CAN'T DO ANYTHING TO SAVE HIM!
PAW!
I GUESS YOU JUST DID HIM A FAVOR, IN YOUR OWN WAY...
LET'S GET OUT OF THIS HELL!

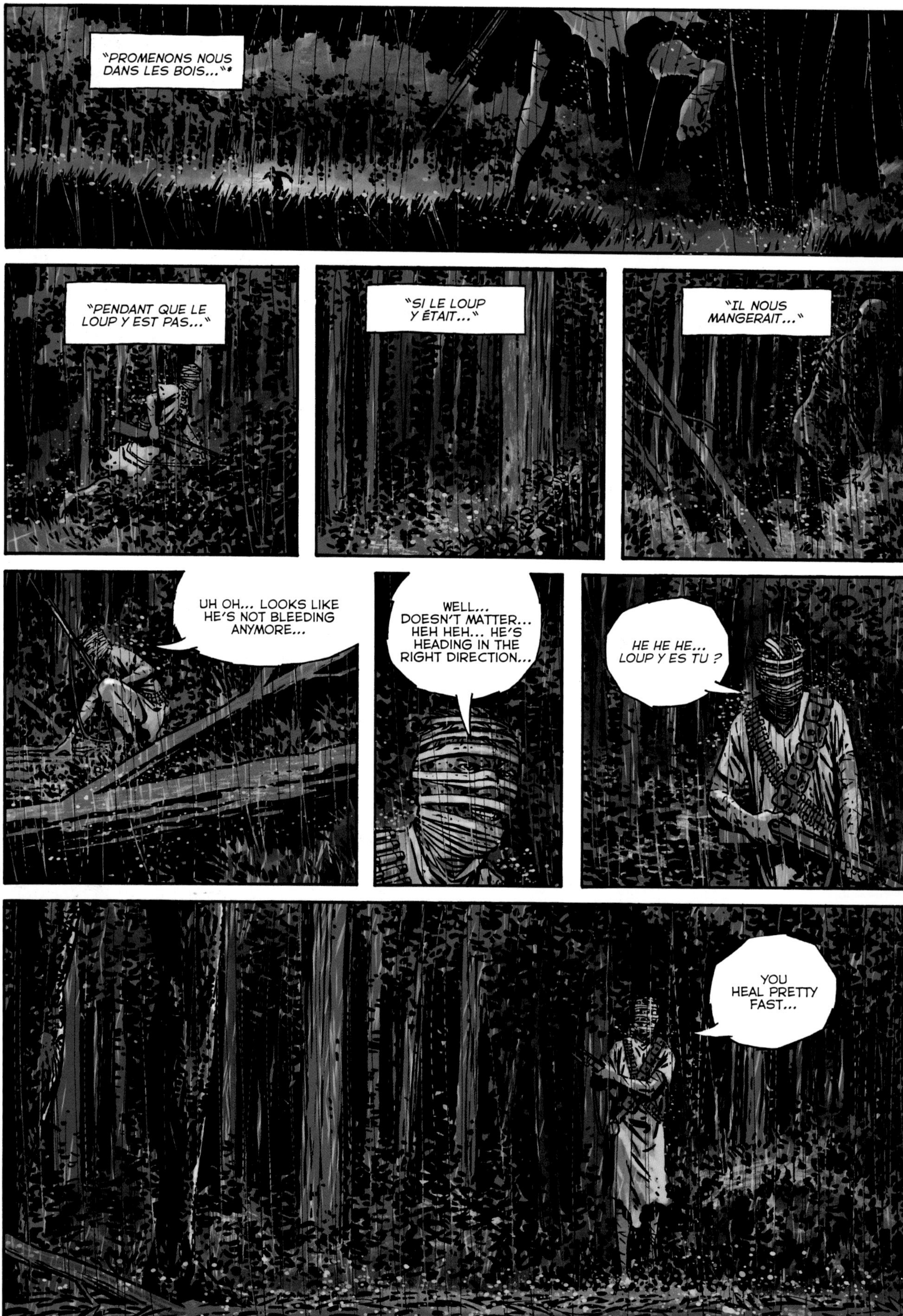
"PROMENONS NOUS DANS LES BOIS..."*
"PENDANT QUE LE LOUP Y EST PAS..."
"SI LE LOUP Y ÉTAIT..."
"IL NOUS MANGERAIT..."
UH OH... LOOKS LIKE HE'S NOT BLEEDING ANYMORE...
WELL... DOESN'T MATTER... HEH HEH... HE'S HEADING IN THE RIGHT DIRECTION...
HE HE HE... LOUP Y ES TU ?
YOU HEAL PRETTY FAST...

*FRENCH CHILDREN'S SONG LYRICS.

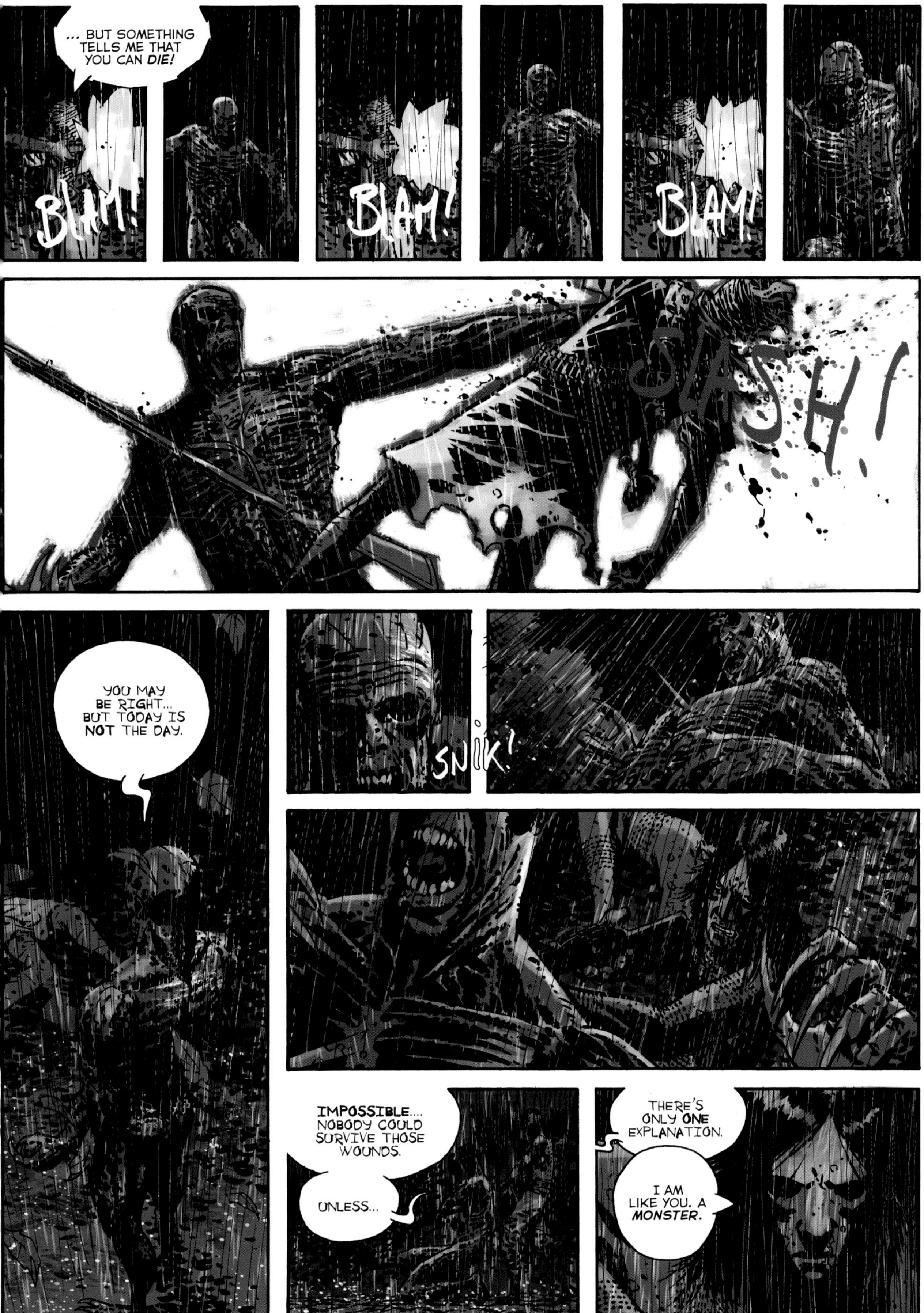
... BUT SOMETHING TELLS ME THAT YOU CAN DIE!
BLAM!
BLAM!
BLAM!
SLASH!
YOU MAY BE RIGHT... BUT TODAY IS NOT THE DAY.
SNIK!
IMPOSSIBLE.... NOBODY COULD SURVIVE THOSE WOUNDS.
UNLESS...
THERE'S ONLY ONE EXPLANATION.
I AM LIKE YOU. A MONSTER.

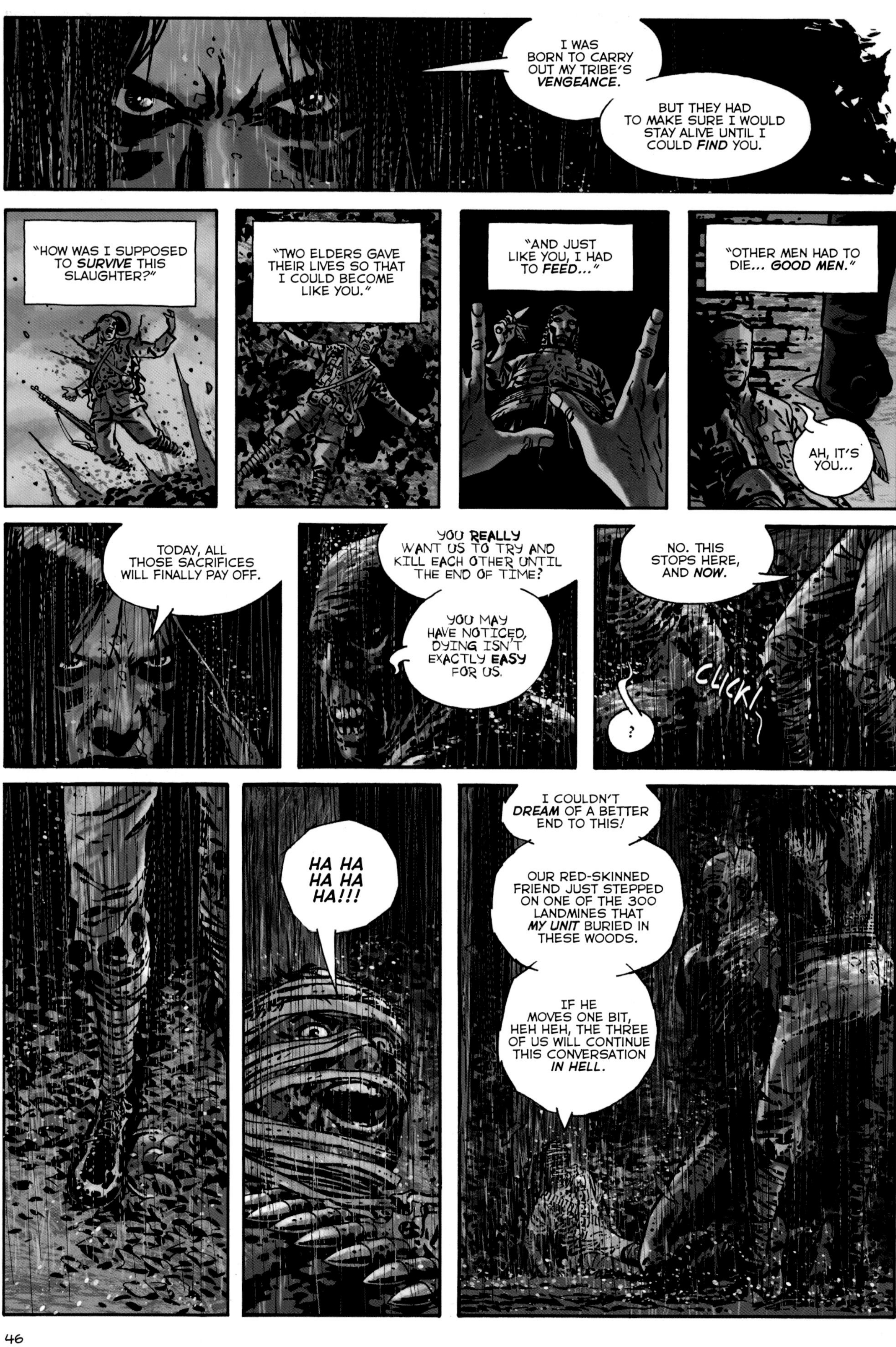
I WAS BORN TO CARRY OUT MY TRIBE'S VENGEANCE.
BUT THEY HAD TO MAKE SURE I WOULD STAY ALIVE UNTIL I COULD FIND YOU.
"HOW WAS I SUPPOSED TO SURVIVE THIS SLAUGHTER?"
"TWO ELDERS GAVE THEIR LIVES SO THAT I COULD BECOME LIKE YOU."
"AND JUST LIKE YOU, I HAD TO FEED..."
"OTHER MEN HAD TO DIE... GOOD MEN."
AH, IT'S YOU...
TODAY, ALL THOSE SACRIFICES WILL FINALLY PAY OFF.
YOU REALLY WANT US TO TRY AND KILL EACH OTHER UNTIL THE END OF TIME?
YOU MAY HAVE NOTICED, DYING ISN'T EXACTLY EASY FOR US.
NO. THIS STOPS HERE, AND NOW.
CLICK!
?
HA HA HA HA HA!!!
I COULDN'T DREAM OF A BETTER END TO THIS!
OUR RED-SKINNED FRIEND JUST STEPPED ON ONE OF THE 300 LANDMINES THAT MY UNIT BURIED IN THESE WOODS.
IF HE MOVES ONE BIT, HEH HEH, THE THREE OF US WILL CONTINUE THIS CONVERSATION IN HELL.

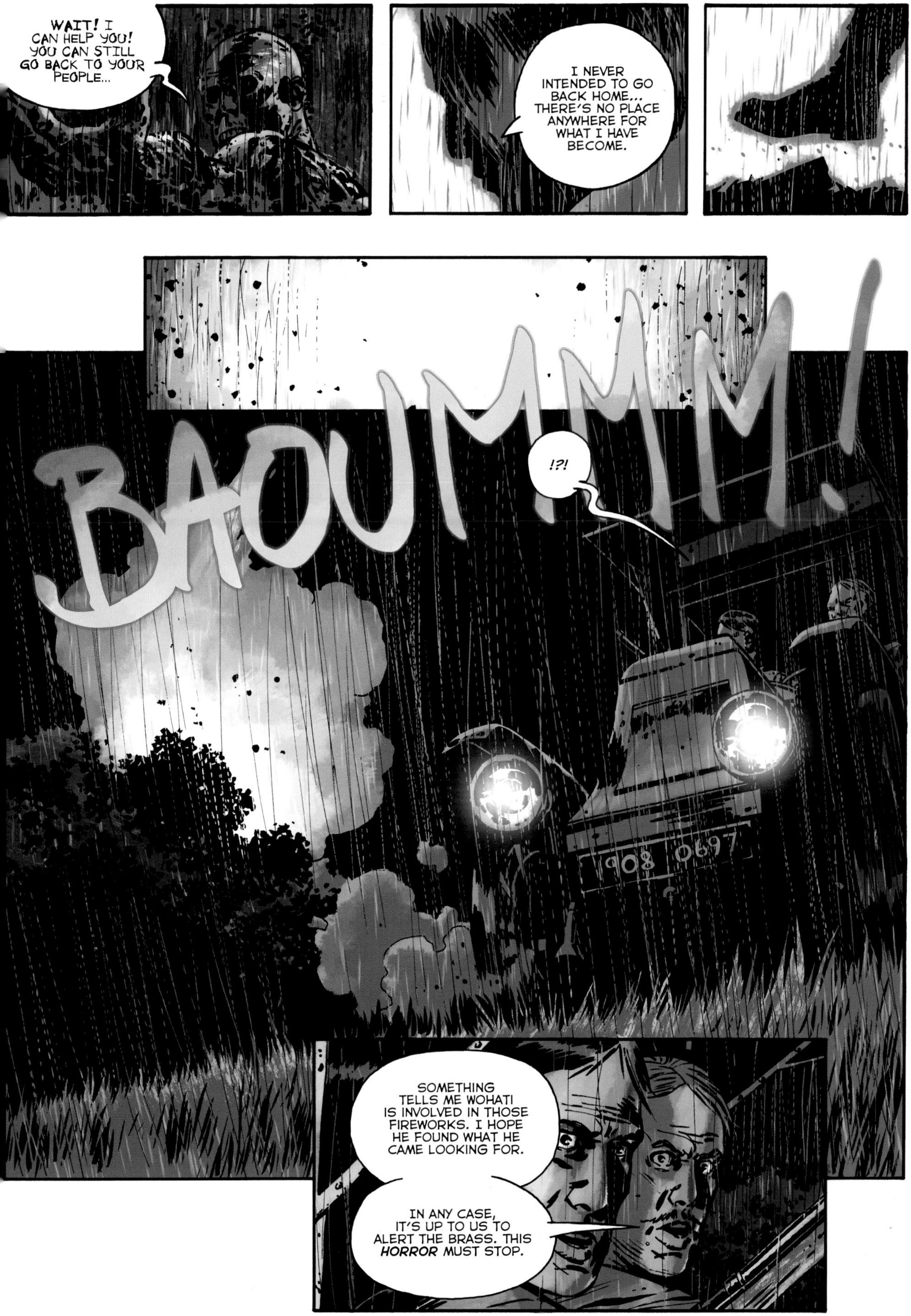

WAIT! I CAN HELP YOU! YOU CAN STILL GO BACK TO YOUR PEOPLE...
I NEVER INTENDED TO GO BACK HOME... THERE'S NO PLACE ANYWHERE FOR WHAT I HAVE BECOME.
BAOUMMMM!
!?!
908 0697
SOMETHING TELLS ME WOHATI IS INVOLVED IN THOSE FIREWORKS. I HOPE HE FOUND WHAT HE CAME LOOKING FOR.
IN ANY CASE, IT'S UP TO US TO ALERT THE BRASS. THIS ***HORROR*** MUST STOP.

OCT 6, 1917 - ARCHIVED REPORTS FROM THE FRENCH COURT MARTIAL. ON THE TRIAL OF SERGEANT LOUIS CHÉREAU, OF THE 146TH INFANTRY REGIMENT, TRIED ON THE CHARGES OF DESERTION, FRATERNIZATION WITH THE ENEMY AND TREASON.

AFTER BEING TAKEN PRISONER BY SCOUTS OF THE 33RD INFANTRY REGIMENT SOME 50 MILES AWAY FROM HIS ASSIGNED POSITION, SGT CHÉREAU WAS UNABLE TO PROVIDE A LEGITIMATE REASON FOR HIS PRESENCE IN THE AREA, NOR WAS HE ABLE TO EXPLAIN HIS DEALINGS WITH THE GERMAN SOLDIER WHO WAS SEEN WITH HIM AND DILLIGENTLY SHOT BY OUR TROUPS.

UNFORTUNATELY, THE COURT WAS UNABLE TO INVESTIGATE SGT CHÉREAU'S RECENT WHEREABOUTS AS HIS SUPERIOR LIEUTENANT RODOLPHE AND THE ENTIRE SECTION UNDER HIS COMMAND WERE FOUND DECEASED IN RECENT ATTEMPTS TO BREAK THROUGH GERMAN LINES.

AFTER TRYING TO LIE TO THE COURT WITH IRRATIONAL ACCOUNTS OF EVENTS THAT WERE CLEARLY FICTITIOUS, SGT CHÉREAU FINALLY AGREED TO CONFESS HIS TREASON AND ADMITTED HIS INSTRUMENTAL ROLE IN HELPING THE ENEMY DISPOSE OF AN ENTIRE SECTION OF THE 11TH INFANTRY REGIMENT, WHICH TO THIS DAY REMAINS UNACCOUNTED FOR.

SGT CHÉREAU ALSO GAVE UP THE POSITION OF A GERMAN BATALLION INFILTRATED BEHIND FRENCH LINES IN THE VILLAGE OF ORIGNY, A POSITION THAT WAS CONFIRMED BY SIGHTINGS OF AT LEAST THREE GERMAN SOLDIERS IN THE VICINITY OF SAID VILLAGE. BASED ON SGT CHÉREAU'S TESTIMONY THAT ALL CIVILIANS HAD BEEN EVACUATED FROM THE AREA, IT WAS DECIDED TO BOMB THE VILLAGE AS A LEGITIMATE MILITARY TARGET.

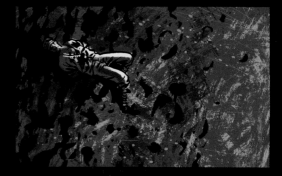

RECON PATROLS SUBSEQUENTLY SENT TO THE VILLAGE FOUND NO SURVIVORS IN THE RUINS; HOWEVER, IT WAS REPORTED THAT A SIGNIFICANT NUMBER OF BODIES WERE WEARING NON-MILITARY CLOTHES. TO THIS DAY, IT REMAINS UNKNOWN AS TO WHY SGT CHÉREAU MIGHT HAVE DELIBERATELY LED TO THE DEATH OF SUCH INNOCENT CIVILIANS. THE ACCUSED WAS SENTENCED TO DEATH ON SEP 14, 1917 AND EXECUTED THE FOLLOWING MORNING.

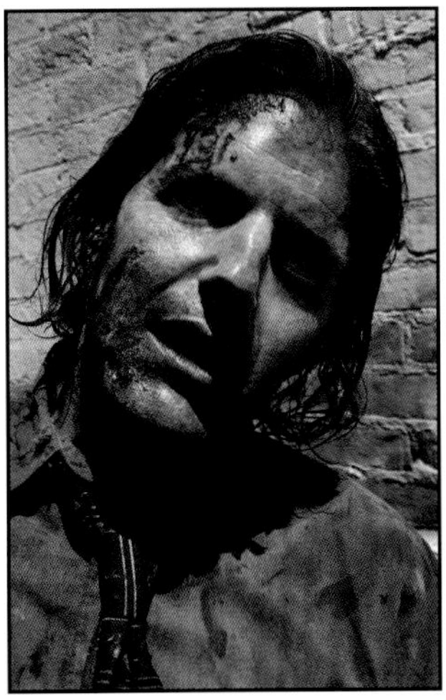

Charlie ADLARD

Interview by Josh Green

You are most well-known for your work as artist on the incredibly popular *The Walking Dead* **series. But first tell me about how you got your start in comics.**

I got my start in comics just like so many other of my contemporaries - just hiking around a portfolio at any con I could get to at the time. It was the mid 80's and I'd just moved back to the town where I was born from London after failed attempts to be a filmmaker (I studied film and video at art college) and a rock star(!) (I play the drums in various bands)... So comics was the last resort.

As soon as I started working again on portfolio stuff and showing it to editors, I realized that it wasn't just a "last resort" but what I was destined to do all my life. It took me roughly two years to break into the industry - I was first hired by the Judge Dredd Megazine - and, to be honest, I haven't looked back since.

The supernatural action in *Curse of the Wendigo* **plays to your strengths as an artist from your work on** *The Walking Dead*. **But just as with** *The Walking Dead*, *Curse of the Wendigo* **is a drama about what defines basic humanity during incredibly cruel times. Did this thematic similarity with** *The Walking Dead* **inspire you to take the artistic assignment for** *Curse of the Wendigo*?

Well, that's certainly one of the reasons that I took on the project. Its themes are very similar and I'm drawn towards more character driven pieces rather than action ones.

But it's also very different, which attracted me. as well.

Whenever I take on a new project outside of the TWD universe, I actively want to distance myself from any major similarities between both - so zombies are definitely out! And I'm reluctant to do horror, as well... But *Wendigo* was such an enticing proposal that I couldn't say no. The horror is very different to TWD... it's much more "off screen" and in the shadows. Plus the historical/reference part really attracted me.

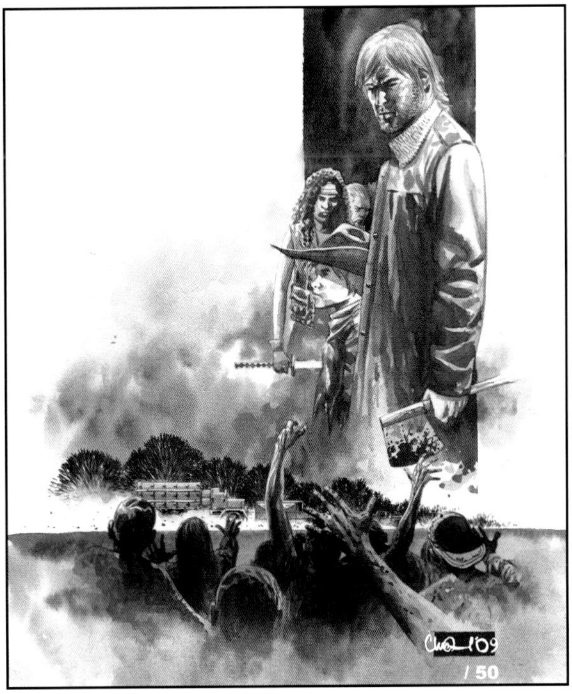
/50

The Walking Dead

Many artists have difficulty maintaining a monthly schedule. Yet month in and out, you produce a new issue of *The Walking Dead*. **Is it difficult working on other projects such as** *Curse of the Wendigo* **concurrently with** *The Walking Dead*? **Also, have you done any artwork outside comics?**

Actually, it's easier sometimes. When I have a monthly schedule, I can work out when I'm finishing each issue and work in

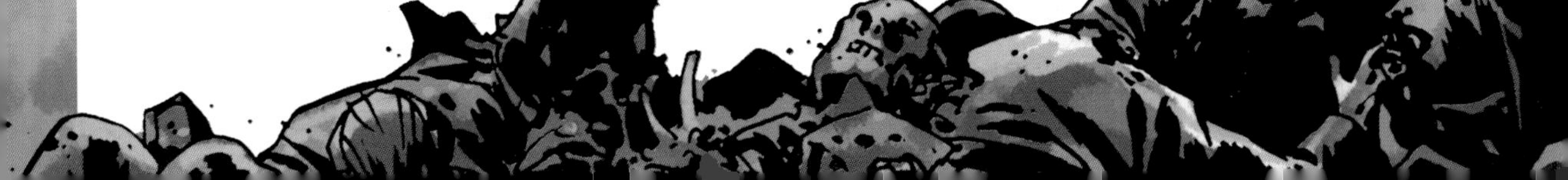

time for other projects accordingly. It takes me roughly 3 weeks to do an issue of TWD - yep, I'm THAT fast - sometimes I have to do issues in 2 weeks... pencils and inks - that can be intense - but it gives me roughly a week per month to work on other stuff. That's how I got *Wendigo* done.

Unfortunately, though, since the advent of the TV show and TWD going stratospheric, I haven't had as much time to do other things. My spare time has been taken up with other TWD projects and a lot more appearances at shows etc. It's frustrating, obviously, since I have a few other projects lined up, which I can't act on yet, but TWD, as long as it lasts, has to be my main focal point and I won't ever ignore that fact.

Regarding other projects outside of comics - there's been a few single illustrations here and there (I did a special Play.com DVD cover to *Diary Of The Dead* and then a film poster to *Survival Of The Dead* for instance) and obviously TWD related stuff, but my heart will always be with comic storytelling and that will always be my main job.

Survival of the Dead

Are there any significant stylistic differences between drawing a European comic such as *Curse of the Wendigo* and American comics like *The Walking Dead*?

Drawing French comics IS quite different to US

ones. The French/Belgium "Bandes Dessines" generally take the form of large format hardcover books around the 48 - 56 page format. The story-telling is much more intense, as you can imagine, since the story is being fitted into generally a one-shot book. Some books get published as series - the average being 3 books - but they tend to be published a year apart... So there has to be a LOT in one volume.

The Walking Dead

With *Wendigo* (as with most other French albums) we went from 5 panels on average per page in TWD to 9 panels for Wendigo... and never stayed on a single scene for more than a couple of pages.

Both formats have their strengths - it's sometimes nice to be quite languid with US comic book story-telling - but, as you might have gathered, I'm a big fan of the European way and it's nice to tackle a different approach now and again.

Doing other projects outside of TWD also enables me to use different equipment too and to experiment more. Again, it's doing stuff like this that keeps me fresh and eager to explore my own artistic horizons even further.

Did you know of Matthieu Missoffe before beginning this assignment? Tell me about your collaborative process with Matthieu. Also, please compare the scripts of Matthieu's *Curse of the Wendigo* to Kirkman's *The Walking Dead*, and how you approached each.

I didn't know Matt before Wendigo - but it was real pleasure working with him.

There weren't any significant differences between Robert's and Matt's scripts - other than the fact that Matt's was in French on one side and English on the other. Thank God he could speak exceptional English... I hope he got paid twice for the translation! I needed the French version too because I was hand drawing the speech balloons, so I needed to size them to the French lettering.

Perhaps the only real difference between the two scripts was that Robert and I are so used to working together that we've developed a kind of script shorthand, whereas *Wendigo* was a first time collaboration, so Matt's script was perhaps a little more detailed, since he wasn't sure how little or how much I might need.

How much research was involved in designing the historical setting and characters in *Curse of the Wendigo*?

There was a lot of research with *Wendigo*. I wanted an authenticity to the book - there had to be. So I spent a long time working on the real settings. Matt helped a great deal - he found me all these old postcards of the village where the climax is set... something I could not find on any search engine on the net.

I firmly believe anyway, that if you draw any book set in the "real" world, it should have "real" things in them... not some fabrication in the artists mind. Which is another reason why I'm attracted to French comics - they seem to put a much greater emphasis on a sense of place as much as the people in their stories, unlike the US/UK, who emphasize the people over place. Just look at *Asterix* and *Tintin* books to see what I mean - fantastically drawn and rendered characters BUT set within a world that's totally real... I can't think of a US equivalent...

On your website, you noted that *Curse of the Wendigo* **is a project that you are incredibly proud of. What makes this stand-out compared to your other accomplishments?**

Yes, I'm very proud of *Wendigo*... But I'm also proud of *Rock Bottom*, *Savage*, *Codeflesh*, *White Death* etc - all of my creator owned projects. I'm proud of them because they're all projects I specifically chose to do and have a deep connection to.

Don't get me wrong - I love TWD too, and it will always be my number one priority, but these are my "special" babies, so to speak! And the advantage to doing something as successful as TWD, is that it pays the bills, so consequentially I can afford to do other projects, not for the money, but because I WANT to do them... It's a good place to be in.

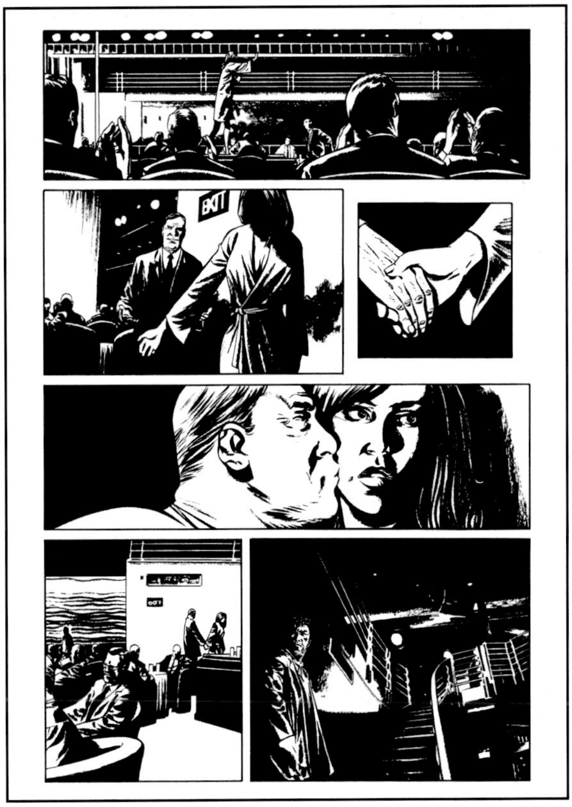
EXIT
Codeflesh

What should fans of yours look forward to in the future outside of *The Walking Dead*? **Perhaps another collaboration with Matthieu?**

I'd love to work with Matt again... But at the moment things are so busy that it'd be a long time off. We're still in touch, so who knows.....?

Regards other projects - there are a few in the pipeline. As I said before, at the moment, I've become a victim of TWD's success, and am not finding the time as I used to to do other things. Having said that, the projects that are in various stages of development (one mostly fully penciled, one with some character sketches, and one just in talks about) are all European comics (well, at least formatted that way), so there'll be plenty more styled comics in the *Wendigo* vein coming from me in the future.

And if I could keep doing TWD into the foreseeable with the odd French album every year or two... I'd be a happy man!

Thanks for letting me speak with you, Charlie, and congratulations on your continued success!

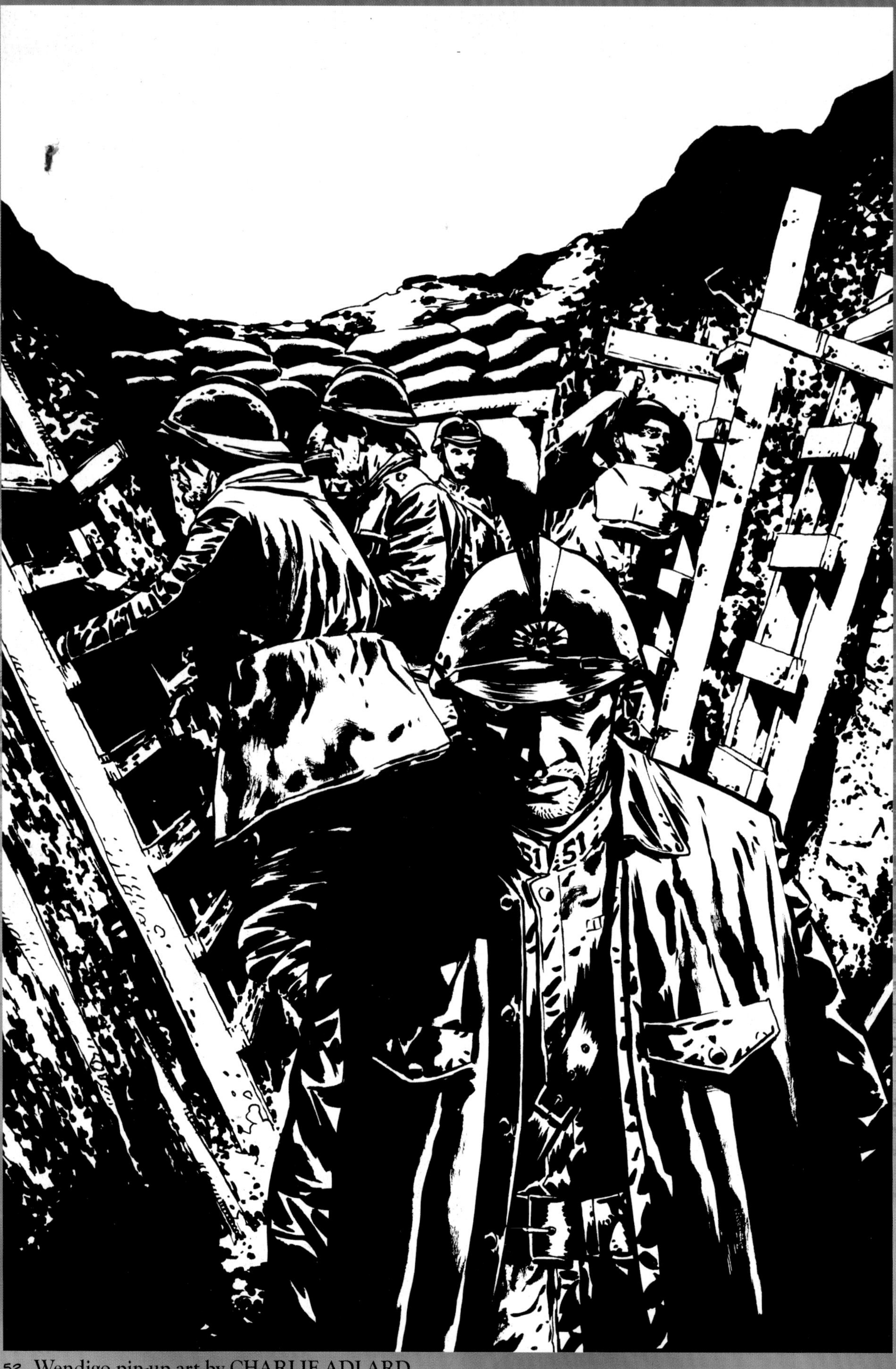

51
51

 Wendigo pin-up art by CHARLIE ADLARD

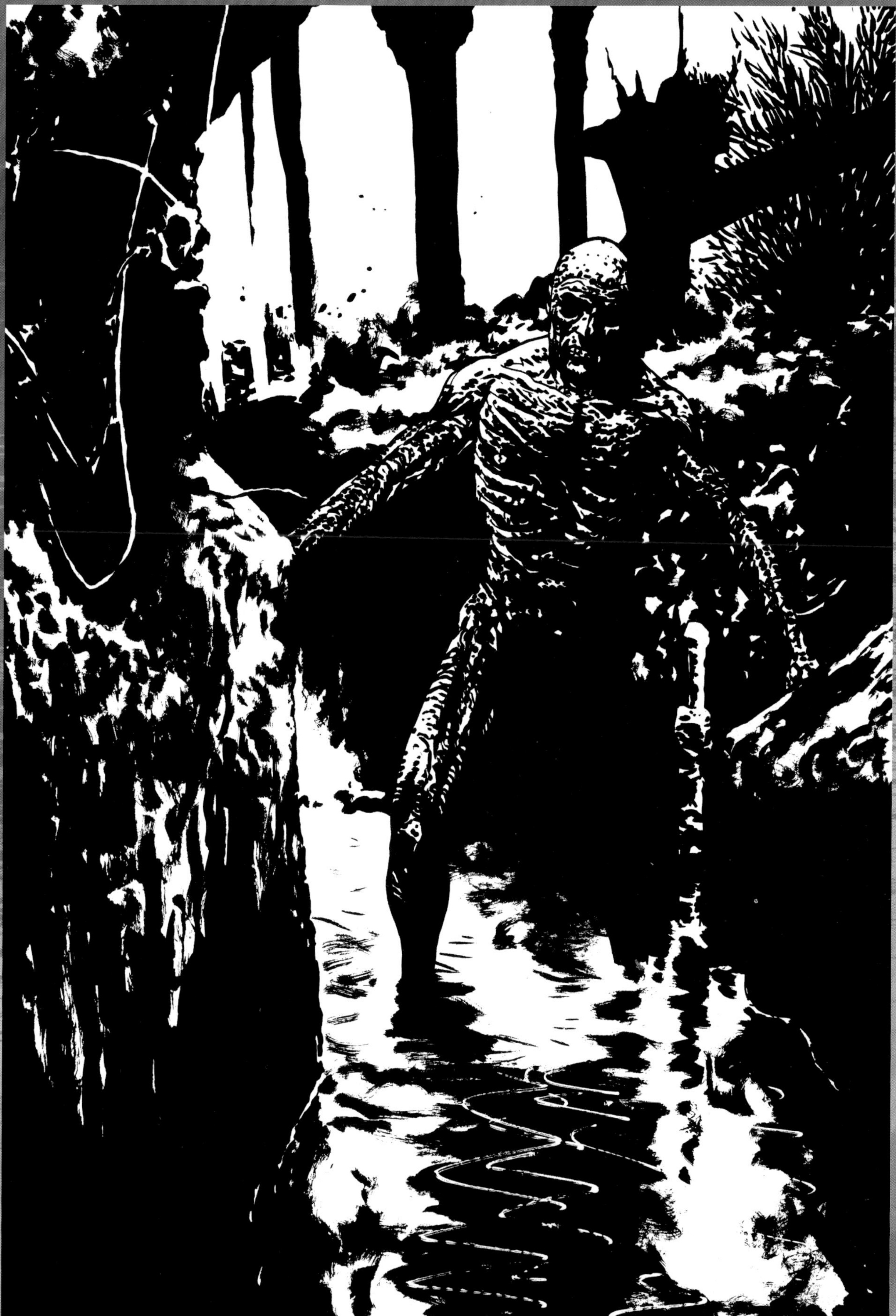

Wendigo pin-up art by CHARLIE ADLARD

Mathieu MISSOFFE

Interview by Josh Green

For Americans unfamiliar with your work, tell me a little about yourself. How did you get your start as a writer? Do you strictly write comic books or do you also write for other mediums?

I worked for a number of years as a development executive for a now defunct TV production company. We were developing a television series for the international market, but the U.S. studios' game is a tough one to crack. So after a couple of pilots didn't get green-lit to series, I decided to give it a shot as a writer. It proved to be a good idea and I am glad I can now share my time between television and comic book projects.

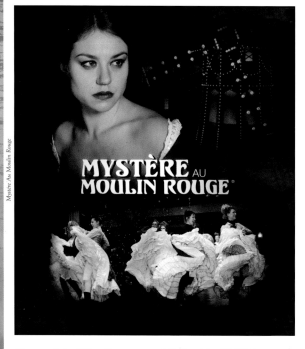

MYSTÈRE AU
MOULIN ROUGE

Mystère Au Moulin Rouge

Curse of the Wendigo was published in 2009 in France by Soleil. Prior to that in 2008, I wrote another book for the same publisher called *Tears in the Sand* (Serge Fino was the graphic artist). It had the same mix of history and supernatural (in this case, "British Desert Rats during WWII opposed to German panzers and mythical Djinns).

Tears in the Sand

When I started working with Charlie Adlard, he was already working with Robert Kirkman on The *Walking Dead*, but I didn't know that particular series. I ordered it online and read it right away. I was really impressed with the scale of the story, the in-depth in character development and of course Charlie's art. As you can imagine, I was immediately excited to work with somebody THAT talented.

With *Curse of the Wendigo* being published in America for the first time, what are your thoughts on American comic books, television programs, and movies?

I am not very impressed with the U.S. studios' current trend to push everything towards family franchises. I understand it makes sense from a financial point of view but the outcome often feels generic (with the exception of anything bat-related, but that's just me).

As far as TV and comic books are concerned, I find that there's an incredible variety of genres being explored, especially the latter, which to me makes them infinitely more interesting both as a creator and viewer/reader. For example, I have been very interested in the various references to classic noir by writers like Bendis, Brubaker, Azzarello, etc... Now it's been done quite a lot, so I am excited to see what's coming next.

Generally speaking, it's probably a mistake to think that every comic book should be turned into a movie or TV series, but it's certainly good news that all these media communicate together. It's clear that having a huge domestic market such as the U.S. allows for greater innovation and risk taking, at least in niche markets. That being said, I am sure the American creative community is as frustrated as any other in the world. Creators vs. marketers... it's the nature of the business.

What inspired you to write *Curse of the Wendigo*?

The book was originally part of a collection of one-shot stories all combining supernatural elements and historical references. Frankly, I don't remember if I had the trenches or the Wendigo first. But I knew for sure what kind of tone I wanted, dark with a touch of "horror survival."

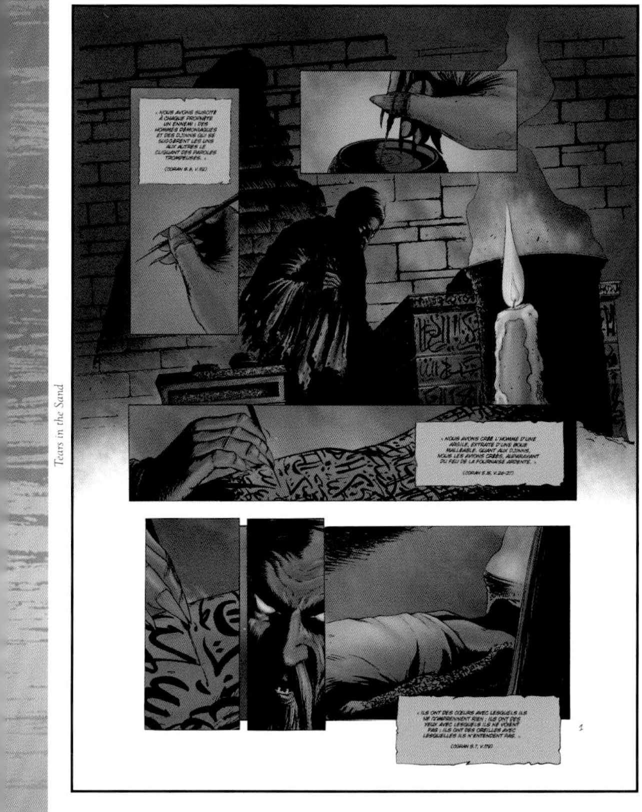
« NOUS AVONS SUSCITÉ À CHAQUE PROPHÈTE UN ENNEMI : DES HOMMES DÉMONIAQUES ET DES DJINNS QUI SE SUGGÈRENT LES UNS AUX AUTRES LE CLIQUANT DES PAROLES TROMPEUSES. »
(CORAN S.6, V.112)
« NOUS AVONS CRÉÉ L'HOMME D'UNE ARGILE, EXTRAITE D'UNE BOUE MALLÉABLE. QUANT AUX DJINNS, NOUS LES AVONS CRÉÉS, AUPARAVANT DU FEU DE LA FOURNAISE ARDENTE. »
(CORAN S.15, V.26-27)

Tears in the Sand

Also, it was really important to me to have a strong human drama element at the core of the story. The unlikely alliance between French and German soldiers was it. There's a well known WWI true story of soldiers ceasing fire to celebrate Christmas together, so I thought taking care of the Wendigo could be another reason for them to temporarily stop killing each other.

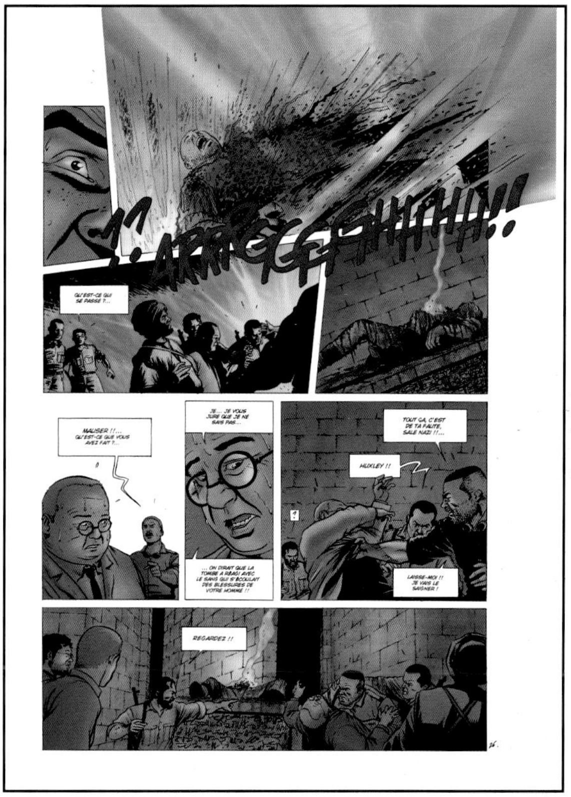
!? ARRRGGGHHHHH!!..
QU'EST-CE QUI SE PASSE ?...
MAUSER !!... QU'EST-CE QUE VOUS AVEZ FAIT ?...
JE... JE VOUS JURE QUE JE NE SAIS PAS...
... ON DIRAIT QUE LA TOMBE A RÉAGI AVEC LE SANG QUI S'ÉCOULAIT DES BLESSURES DE VOTRE HOMME !!
TOUT ÇA, C'EST DE TA FAUTE, SALE NAZI !!...
HUXLEY !!
LAISSE-MOI !! JE VAIS LE SAIGNER !
REGARDEZ !!

Tears in the Sand

At the end of the day the trickiest part was definitely to make everything fit in 46 pages, which is quite short. Every writer on Earth knows it's the toughest part of the job, and I didn't want to sacrifice anything: action, character work, atmosphere etc...

Comic book readers often read stories dealing with the supernatural, but what made you want to set this particular story during WWI?

I think WWI naturally lends itself to that kind of story, and I had already screened a few horror movies set in that time period.

First, the trenches provide for a great claustrophobic atmosphere, isolating characters from each other and from the rest of the world. Charlie did a superb job with this environment, and his use of actual pictures really strengthens the whole thing.

Equally important, if not more, were the symbolic aspects of the conflict. To this day, WWI carries in Europe a very distinctive image of mindless butchery and War in general has always been a good, classic metaphor for cannibalism. It feeds on men just like the Wendigo, and without too much headache, you can even see that the end of the 19th and beginning of the 20Th century introduced us to a whole new "modern" system often described as another form of cannibalism (so the Wendigo basically supports Socialist thinking, I guess...).

How familiar were you with the myths of the Wendigo and the history of World War I when preparing this story? How intensive was your research?

WWI was easy as I only used well-known images and school book facts, but things got a lot tougher with the part on the Wendigo and its actual roots in Native American folklore.

I knew I wanted the whole thing to feel "real," or as realistic as possible, so I set out to find out as much as possible on the specific myth of the Wendigo and the Cree tribes where it originated.

The connection with potential early Viking visitors is obviously something I made up, but I was very interested to find out that there were actual accounts of people resorting to cannibalism under what they believed to be the influence of the spirit of the Wendigo, and that these accounts had been studied in-depth from a psychiatric point of view. I have always been fascinated by the tricks of the mind and the science around them, so I created the part with the two doctors in the mental institution which fits well with the period as those years were important for the fairly new field of psychiatry. This is typically the kind of things I would have never thought of without the research, and I am very glad it came up.

The revelation of Wohati's actions were shocking to say the least. He was forced to do some truly horrible acts. Did you struggle with writing such a complicated protagonist for this story?

That particular twist (the fact that Wohati is himself a Wendigo) also came up late in the writing process. At first I had thought that his quest across the world to kill the Wendigo was enough to make him a true hero in the reader's mind. But then I thought about how little chance he had to survive in the war before even meeting his target, so it started to make sense that he would use his tribe's magic to better the odds. And only then did I realize that Wohati's real act of bravery was his sacrifice: he gave up his humanity to make sure he would succeed in his duty. That's when he became more of a tragic hero in my mind, with the notion that this whole adventure was always meant to be a one-way trip for him.

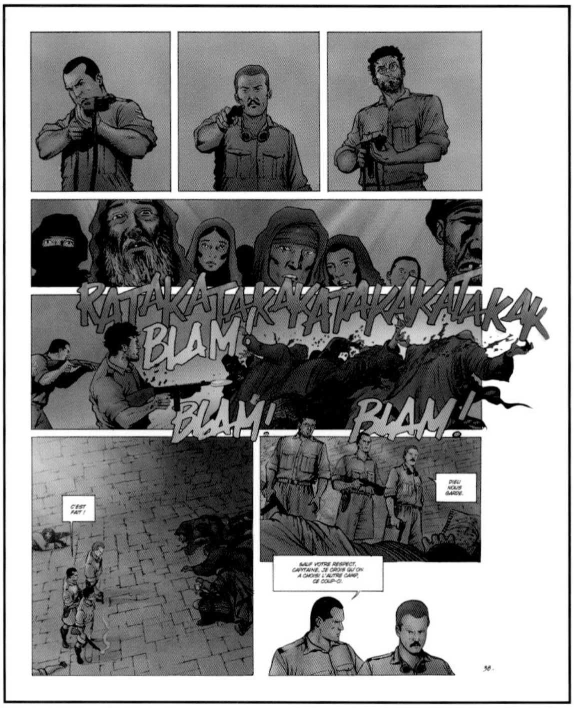
BLAM!
BLAM!
BLAM!
C'EST FAIT !
DIEU NOUS GARDE.
SAUF VOTRE RESPECT, CAPITAINE, JE CROIS QU'ON A CHOISI L'AUTRE CAMP, CE COUP-CI.
38.
Tears in the Sand

Do you plan on revisiting the WWI time period or use similar supernatural elements in upcoming stories, whether they be for comic books or television programs?

I am not sure about WWI or the Wendigo per se but I have always liked the idea of setting stories in different historical settings so I guess I'm bound to doing it again. Whatever time period you choose, the past is always an exotic location, and it is also a great opportunity to put today's world into perspective.

What TV Shows and comic book projects do you have coming up in the pipeline?

I recently wrote a TV Movie called "Mystery at the Moulin Rouge," co-written with Elsa Marpeau and directed by Stephane Kappes. It was definitely meant to have a mainstream feeling, but I really enjoyed merging a modern "Jack The Ripper" kind of thriller within the golden years of the Moulin Rouge.

Otherwise I am working on a comic book project based on the famous French Novel "Les Miserables," and a fantasy/horror story set in a controversial behavioral modification school program.

It was a pleasure, Matthieu!